D1823466

Preparing For
The Coming Spiritual Outpouring
Reflections On The Coming Move Of God's Spirit

by R. Maurice Smith

RISING
RIVER
MEDIA

© Copyright 2011, Rising River Media. All rights reserved.

Written permission must be secured from the publisher to use or reproduce any part of this work in any form except where quotations are accompanied by a full and accurate recitation of the work's full title, the publisher, and the publisher's address. Additional copies of this publication are available from the addresses given below:

Published by Rising River Media, P. O. Box 18793, Spokane, Washington 99228

www.safehousesofhopeandprayer.org

Cover design & original art work by Gale A. Smith.
Cover photo and inside art licensed through istock.

All Scripture quotations from *The New American Standard Bible* (© Copyright 1960, 1962, 1963, 1968, 1972, 1973, 1975, 1977, The Lockman Foundation, La Habra, California) unless otherwise indicated.

ISBN 13   978-0-9815289-2-2

ISBN 10   0-9815289-2-9

Other Titles Available From Rising River Media

All Dogs Go To Heaven, Don't They? *Biblical Reflections On Christian Universalism and Ultimate Reconciliation*

River Houses Rising *The Rise of Safe Houses Of Hope And Prayer*

Safe Houses of Hope And Prayer
Your Practical Guide To the House Church Revolution

The Least of These *The Role of Good Deeds In A Jesus-Shaped Spirituality*

The Inextinguishable Blaze *God's Call To Holiness, Repentance, Intimacy and Spiritual Awakening*

When Jesus Visit's His Church *Studies In The Seven Churches of Revelation*

You Wanna Do What In Your House?! *Straight Answers To Your Most Frequently Asked Questions About House Church*

All titles are available on our website at

www.safehousesofhopeandprayer.org

and through Amazon.com!

Table of Contents

Author's Reflections

On the eve of the great Welsh Revival of 1904, Evan Roberts wrote to Mr Harley Aspden, the Editor of the **Sunday Companion** asking for a cost quotation for printing some *"Revival Picture Post-cards"*. At the end of his letter he added these words, *"We are on the eve of a great and grand revival, the greatest the world has ever seen. Do not think that the writer is a madman"*. The world now knows that Evan Roberts was no madman, and by the end of the month in which he wrote that letter the great Welsh Revival of 1904 was underway. What most people are unaware of is the fact that Evan Roberts, by his own admission, had been praying for revival for nearly 13 years.

In my personal Journal for the year 2002-2003 I opened with the following entry:

December 15, 2002 - *"I believe this will prove to be an unusual Journal, for I believe that within its pages will be recorded the beginnings of a great outpouring of God's Spirit in the Pacific Northwest, beginning in Spokane. Or it will record why the Church in Spokane was unable and unwilling to give birth to a new movement of God. Time will tell which of these two outcomes came to pass."*

Now, nearly 10 years later, we are still awaiting the outcome. Personally, I continue to believe that we, today, are standing on the eve of the greatest spiritual outpouring the Church has experienced in well over 100 years. The River of God's Spirit, the River of Ezekiel 47, is about to flow in spiritual power and blessing unknown in the experience of our generation (as well as the generation of our fathers and grand-fathers). Furthermore, it is an outpouring that will flow through new channels, namely, through simple, organic house churches and other non-institutional structures where God is met on His terms, not ours.

The purpose of this book is to encourage you to think, to pray and to prepare for what God is about to do. This coming

Preparing For A Spiritual Outpouring

outpouring will be unlike anything you or I have ever experienced. Over the past several years God has spoken to me from time to time about what He intends to do, and I have tried to "chronicle my thoughts and reflections via my weekly e-letters which I send out to friends and subscribers. Because I believe that this spiritual outpouring is very near, and because I believe God has given me some small degree of insight into it, I have decided to bring many of those newsletters together into one "volume" as a way of summarizing what God has been saying over the past six years. In the process of compiling and preparing this booklet I have tried to resist the temptation to add to (or subtract from) what I originally said, choosing instead to keep the primary articles more-or-less intact with only minor editorial changes where I felt it appropriate.

My goal for this booklet is to communicate the overall sense of what God has been saying and doing as He prepares us for the coming spiritual outpouring. My prayer is that you will find these thoughts helpful as you pray and prepare for what God is about to do in our midst.

I believe that recent events have highlighted the need for God's people to intentionally prepare for a coming season of spiritual outpouring. Indeed, outward signs of revival should encourage us to pray and seek God for more. May the faithful prayers of all those saints who have fasted and prayed for revival in Spokane and our nation for many years soon find their fulfillment in a season of divine visitation when the River of God's Spirit, the River of Ezekiel 47, flows in breath-taking power through our homes and our communities, and through the Church which meets in your house.

 Let the River flow!

Maurice Smith
Rising River Media
Advent, 2011

Of Wells, Battleships & Memorials

First Published January 7, 2003

1

And A Season Begins . . . .

"I can hear that thunder in the distance,
It's like a train on the edge of the town;
I can feel the brooding of Your Spirit,
Lay your burdens down,
Lay your burdens down."

As I began the return trip from my Christmas holiday with family in North Carolina I noticed something . . . unusual. About mid-way home, somewhere between Atlanta and Seattle, I began to sense a growing burden and groaning in my spirit. I commented to my wife on the plane that it was as if the burden was growing as we approached the Pacific Northwest (PNW). There is a groaning in the Spirit over this area. And it is growing. I believe that we in Spokane and the PNW are entering into a new Season of God's dealings which I believe will begin to unfold over the next six months. The River of Ezekiel 47, the River of God's Spirit, is building in preparation to flow in power and blessing unprecedented in our generation. Are we prepared for what is about to be unleashed upon His Church?

Of Wells, Battleships & Memorials

To prepare for new battles (and blessings) I believe in remembering and learning from old ones. Why? Because God has a habit of repeating Himself, just never in the same way twice. So bear with me while I remember . . . and prepare you for what is about to come.

Upon arriving home in Fayetteville I sensed God saying that I should pay a visit to UNC-Chapel Hill where I attended college. I shared in my last E-Letter Update (yes, you really should read it if you haven't) how God moved on that campus in the mid-1970s as a result of fasting & prayer and the efforts of the various campus ministries which laid down their individual

9

Preparing For A Spiritual Outpouring

agendas in order to work and pray together for God's Kingdom purposes. As I walked the campus I remembered the all-night prayer gatherings, evangelistic dorm meetings, speakers in fraternity & sorority houses, leading my roommate to Christ after he and the others in my dorm "forced" me to let them watch an evangelistic movie sent to me by the Billy Graham Association. I remembered the hours I spent alone in The Chapel of the Cross (an Episcopal Chapel on the edge of campus that remained open all night for prayer) interceding for the campus known around North Carolina as a "hot-bed of communist insurgency" (according to a local WRAL commentator by the name of Jesse Helms). Before leaving I took the family to pose for pictures at "The Old Well" the symbolic center of campus. As I sent them on ahead to a local restaurant for lunch I stayed and began to pray there at "The Old Well." As I prayed I began to weep as I sensed God saying that there are no cold and spiritually hard places, only places where His Presence has not come. His Presence is coming. Are we prepared? Are we prepared to lay down our personal or corporate agendas in order to fast and pray and labor together for His Kingdom Purposes in our area?

My next "pilgrimage" was to the coast of North Carolina. I sensed that I should take the family down to Wilmington to visit the U.S.S. North Carolina Battleship Memorial. Now there is literally a history here. The U.S.S.N.C. was commissioned in 1941 and was one of the largest battleships afloat at that time. It fought in every major naval engagement of the Pacific War, was torpedoed, repaired and fought again. In short, it was the "hero" of the Pacific War. But in the late 1940s it was decommissioned and in the late 1950s the Navy announced that it would be sold for scrap. I was in the 1st grade when we learned that a plan had been hatched to save the North Carolina. Thousands of school children from across the State collected dimes (well, a dime was silver then and actually worth something!) in order to save the Battleship. The plan was successful. The State bought the ship and it is now safely moored in Wilmington as a floating memorial to the men who fought and died in the Pacific during World War 2.

Chapter 1 - Of Wells Battleships & Memorials

A visit to the Memorial is an awe-inspiring event for any student of history. The war in the Pacific was fought and won by ships like this and by the brave crews who risked their very lives to win obscure-but-critical battles now forgotten. As I toured the Memorial I was struck by several thoughts and comparisons. The problem with a Memorial is . . . that it is a Memorial. The U.S.S. NC is no longer a Battleship except in name. It is now a memorial to past victories, not a weapon of war for future battles. Furthermore, it's brave crew is gone, present only in the form of an Honor Roll listing those who once served, fought, died and triumphed. They have been replaced now with tourists whose only real risk is that of running out of camera batteries before the tour is done.

Forgive me for a harsh comparison, but here it comes. Much of the organized & institutional Church in America and the West is like the U.S.S. North Carolina; a stately and beautiful Memorial to past battles fought and won, but not a weapon of war for the spiritual battles that now confront us as individuals, as churches and as a civilization. And our congregants & attendees resemble middle class vacationers in search of the concession stand more than they resemble soldiers prepared for fighting battles and winning great victories. Just as we wouldn't tow the U.S.S.N.C. out to do naval battle today, so much of the visible church in its present state is in no condition to confront and fight the spiritual battles that inevitably surround revival and God's Kingdom purposes. It is a memorial to past battles, not a weapon of war for future ones.

Revival Is Coming

So, what does all of this mean (other than the obvious, that Maurice did a lot of sight-seeing over Christmas!)? Let me summarize. Revival is coming. I have sensed this burden before, and it is growing. The River of Ezekiel 47 is building, preparing to flow in power and blessing unknown in our generation. While the Pacific Northwest has traditionally been known as a spiritually cold and hard place (not unlike a certain University campus of my acquaintance), the Lord declares that

Preparing For A Spiritual Outpouring

there are no spiritually hard or cold places, only places where His Presence has not yet come. And He is coming. His coming will require that each of us lay down our personal and/or corporate agendas in order to fast, pray and labor together for His Kingdom purposes of our area. And He is raising up new channels and new vessels for the flow of His River, vessels known as house churches or simple churches. And He is raising up people and simple churches willing to fight the spiritual battles and confront the spiritual strongholds that always accompany or are revealed by any great move of God's Spirit. This battle cannot be fought and won by Memorials to yesterday, or by tourists more concerned with comfort than with battle. And this coming outpouring of God's Presence will have two great effects. First, it will renew, redeem and empower the true Church of God, the Body and Bride of His Son. She will once again be beautiful. Second, it will result in the Spirit convicting the world of sin, righteousness and judgment, just as Jesus promised (John 16:8).

So, there you have it. There is a certain risk in sharing all of this with you. It is possible that all of this vision concerning revival is, in the words of C. H. Spurgeon, nothing more than *"the steam from an overheated brain."* After all, in recent years the predicting of a coming revival has become somewhat of a cottage industry, including full page newspaper ads and billboards. But as I said earlier, I have sensed this burden before, and it is growing beyond anything in my experience. What is coming will not be defined as an event, a program, a meeting, a crusade, festival or anything man-produced (although all of those things may occur at some point). It will be remembered as a River of God's Presence and Power that flowed through our families, our churches and our community.

He is coming. Are we ready? Is your House Church a channel through which He can flow?

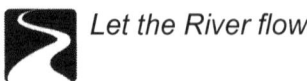 *Let the River flow!*

Church Growth And
A Season of Repentance

2

First Published October 16, 2003

I want to begin by discussing the difference between a season of God's activity and a church growth program. I recently made an observation on our daily radio program that, in my opinion, much of the modern day church growth movement is little more than a man-made substitute for God's church growth program which is revival. I have studied the history of revivals going back 500 years to the beginning of the Protestant Reformation, and I can tell you with absolute confidence that the times and seasons of the church's greatest growth (in terms of raw numbers, percentages of the population and the quality of the long term-results) have occurred during times of revival when the River of God's Spirit flowed through communities and nations in such power that people were swept into the Kingdom of God because of an overwhelming sense of the Presence of God (You and I call those times "revival").

Stories To Illustrate

Let me tell you a story to illustrate this point. During the 1830s and 40s in America there was a powerful outpouring of the River of God's Spirit, particularly in the New England area. The most prominent evangelist in America during that period of time was Charles Grandison Finney. On one occasion during this season of God's outpouring Finney was preaching in a town in New York when he was invited by some Christian employees at a local cotton factory to lead a small bible study group in prayer. When Finney arrived at the factory he proceeded to walk across the factory floor to where the bible study was to be held. As he passed through the factory, workers on the factory floor began to weep under a powerful conviction of sin. Soon, many of the workers were weeping and unable to work. The factory owner was not a Christian. But when he realized what was happening he closed the factory, saying *"Souls are more important than business."* He then invited Finney to preach to the assembled workers. Finney preached, and when he finished nearly every worker in the factory professed Christ as savior.

Let me illustrate this again. In 2002 Spokane hosted an excellent Franklin Graham Festival which averaged 20,000 per night at the 4 day series of meetings. There were probably close to 500 area churches represented by the attendees at the Festival. If you divided the nightly attendance by the number of churches represented you would have roughly 40 people per church. That's not really a lot of people per church and its hardly a revival. But during the Welsh revival of 1904 every church in Wales was filled to capacity 7 nights per week, some of them 24 hours a day, for over 6 months! You see, that's the difference between a season of divine visitation and an evangelistic program. Do you think all of those people in Wales who thronged the churches 7 days a week, 24 hours a day for 6 months or longer were coming because the churches had suddenly become seeker sensitive and were placing their songs & messages into power point presentations? Of course not. They were coming because the Presence of God was there. You see, in a season of God's visitation it's like living beneath an open window in heaven, and it is God Who draws people to himself and it's the Holy Spirit who convicts them of sin, righteousness and judgment.

During the Manhattan Prayer Revival of 1857 there are stories of ships at sea (two ships in particular, the U.S.S Virginia and the U.S.S. North Carolina) and as the ships approached New York Harbor the men on board became overwhelmed with a sense of God's Presence and their own sin and need for Christ. As soon as the ships docked the men all headed for churches on shore! In the Welsh Revival of 1904 there are documented stories of people walking into bars, ordering a drink and then being unable to drink it, setting it down, leaving the bar and gong to the nearest church to find Christ. Taverns went bankrupt due to the loss of business. In some jurisdictions crime all but disappeared and some judges were issued white gloves signifying no cases to try. That's what it's like to experience a season of God's visitation in revival. It's like living

Chapter 2 - Church Growth

beneath an open window in heaven.

God's Desperation Plan For Church Growth

You see, I believe that God wants church growth even more than we do. He just has a different plan for how to do it. God's plan is what I call "the desperation plan." God wants His church to become so desperate regarding its condition, that it is willing to acknowledge and own up to its own failure and spiritual bankruptcy, so that when He moves to sweep people into His church the praise and the glory will belong to him alone. Revival comes when the people of God begin to pray the prayers of desperate people who have come face to face with their own spiritual poverty and failure. Do you want to know why God hasn't sent revival yet? Because we are not yet broken, humble and desperate. We still have one more new seeker-relevant church growth book to read or conference to attend that could be the magic bullet to mega-church growth, and we're still convinced that, if we can just get the formula right, ours can be the next seeker-driven community mega church that Christianity Today or Charisma magazine will feature on their cover.

I believe that God wants to open a window over our area and initiate a season of His divine activity that will see His church renewed and empowered, and will see our community transformed. The question is: How do we get there? As I said at the beginning of this article, I have been struggling with this question for the past month (or longer). What I have sensed is that at this point in time, in this present season, God wants His Church to face up to the reality of its own sins and abysmal failure and to enter into a season of repentance. Scripture says, *"The sacrifices of God are a broken spirit; a broken and a contrite heart, O God, Thou wilt not despise."* (Psalm 51:17) In other words, brokenness, contrition and humility are always good before God; everything else is suspect.

I believe God is calling His Church into a season of brokenness, humility, contrition, confession and repentance for

Preparing For A Spiritual Outpouring

its sin. In the immortal words of Pogo: "We have seen the enemy, and he is us"! I believe that it is time for the Church to acknowledge that WE ARE the stronghold of the enemy. WE ARE the reason revival tarries and church growth languishes.

In the process of thinking and praying through this issue of a season of repentance I have been struck (again) by the biblical role of fasting in the process of repentance. If God is indeed leading His Church (at least that portion of it that is willing and responsive to what He is calling us to do) into a season of repentance, then we must consider the biblical steps involved in seeking God for His will in such a season.

"And with fasting let us always join in fervent prayer, pouring out our whole souls before God, confessing our sins with all their aggravations, humbling ourselves under his mighty hand, laying open before him all our wants, all our guiltiness and helplessness. This is a season for enlarging our prayers, both in behalf of ourselves and of our brethren. Let us now bewail the sins of our people, and cry aloud for the city of our God: that the Lord may build up Zion, and cause his face to shine on her desolations."

As one of the leaders of the First Great Awakening in England, Wesley understood the important role fasting plays in confession of sin and preparation for revival. As we enter this new season of God's dealings with His church in Spokane and our area, a season of preparation for revival, one of the crying needs of the church in our relationship with God is to enter into a season of earnest repentance for our sins. And biblically, fasting is supposed to play an important role in how the church deals with its own sin. When we look at the Old Testament we see the people of God practicing fasting in order to deal with their sin in four ways:

1. They fasted in order to humble themselves before God.
In 1 Peter 5:5-6 Peter exhorts elders to *"clothe yourselves with humility toward one another, for God is opposed to the proud, but gives grace to the humble. Humble yourselves therefore*

Chapter 2 - Church Growth

under the mighty hand of God . . ." The Old Testament mentality was very practical and concrete. Fasting, as taught and practiced in the Old Testament, provides a practical means for us to humble ourselves before God and one another. There is a clear scriptural relationship between humbling ourselves and fasting. In Leviticus 16:31 God instructed the Israelites to "afflict" their souls each year on the Day of Atonement. The Hebrew word translated "afflict" in Leviticus 16:31 means "to be bowed down or afflicted." It is the same word which is translated "humble" in Psalm 35:13 where David declared, "I humbled my soul with fasting." The same word is found along with fasting context in several passages, including Ezra 8:21 where Ezra proclaimed a fast, "that we might humble ourselves." The word for "fast" and "humble" are used together. In Scripture, fasting is God's appointed means for believers to "afflict" their souls and to humble themselves before God, demonstrating our earnestness and sincerity of purpose in confronting sin in our lives. Another famous passage that refers to believers humbling themselves is found in 2 Chronicles 7:14 - here Solomon declared "if My people who are called by My name humble themselves and pray, and seek my face and turn from their wicked ways, then I will hear from heaven, will forgive their sin, and will heal their land." This verse is often quoted with reference to the requirements for revival. It is, in fact, a call for the people of God to humble themselves with fasting and prayer in order to turn from their sins and to experience revival. In the Old Testament, Fasting is a discipline of the body which has a tendency to humble the soul. If we want to experience the revival and renewal (the word used is "to heal) promised by 2 Chronicles 7:14, then perhaps we need to follow the biblical pattern of humility. Perhaps it is time for the church to humble itself before its God in fasting. In the words of Arthur Wallis:

"If you have been brought low through personal defeat; if there is a call in your soul to a deeper purifying, to a renewed consecration; if there is the challenge of some new task for which you feel ill equipped - then it is time to inquire of God whether He would have you separate yourself unto Him in fasting."

Preparing For A Spiritual Outpouring

2. They Fasted As A Means of Confessing Their Sins. The relationship between fasting and the confession of sin can be powerfully seen in Ezra 9:5ff, "But at the evening offering I arose from my humiliation, even with my garment and my robe torn, and I fell on my knees and stretched out my hands to the Lord my God; and I said, 'O my God, I am ashamed and embarrassed to lift up my face to Thee, my God, for our iniquities have risen above our heads, and our guilt has grown even to the heavens.'" The Hebrew word translated "humiliation" here means "to afflict or humble oneself by fasting." The remainder of the chapter is Ezra's confession of the people's sin and his prayer for God's forgiveness. The result of Ezra's fasting and confession was that a spirit of conviction over sin began to spread among the people, *"Now while Ezra was praying and making confession, weeping and prostrating himself before the house of God, a very large assembly, men, women, and children, gathered to him from Israel; for the people wept bitterly"* (Ezra 10:1). Ezra's time of fasting, humiliation and confession of sin had a powerful effect upon the people of Israel, resulting in their own conviction, confession, mourning (as evidenced by their "weeping bitterly") and repentance from sin. God intends for times of personal and corporate fasting to be times of acknowledging and confessing our sins, confessing them first before God and secondly before those persons against whom we have sinned.

3. They Fasted In Order To Mourn Their Sins. In the Old Testament there is also a relationship between fasting and mourning. In the passage from Ezra 10 referred to above the word "mourning" is found in verse 6, *"Then Ezra rose from before the house of God and went into the chamber of Jehohanan the son of Eliashib. Although he went there, he did not eat bread, nor drink water, for he was mourning over the unfaithfulness of the exiles."* Here the relationship is clear between fasting ("he did not eat . . . nor drink") and mourning. Ezra fasted as an expression of mourning over the sin of the people. Ezra didn't simply confess his sin and the sins of the people as some form of "intellectual agreement" with God. It went much deeper. As a result of his fasting, Ezra's heart was

Chapter 2 - Church Growth

broken by the sins which broke the heart of God. It is one thing to intellectually and mentally acknowledge our sin and to confess it. It is quite another when God touches our heart and causes it to break over our sin, just as His heart breaks over our sin. Ezra expressed his mourning by fasting, but his fasting led to a deeper mourning because his heart had been broken over sin. We see the relationship again in Nehemiah 1:4, *"Now it came about when I heard these words, I sat down and wept and mourned for days; and I was fasting and praying before the God of heaven."* Here we see fasting that results specifically in mourning and weeping over sin (the sin is specified in Nehemiah's prayer for forgiveness in verse 7). In the Old Testament, fasting is a form of mourning, particularly mourning for one's sins. Biblical mourning is neither the self-centered remorse nor the hopeless grief of the unbeliever. Instead, biblical mourning through fasting is a response to the prompting of the Holy Spirit through which we share in a small measure in God's own grief over our sin. Fasting is a time when we consider and mourn our own sins, failures and shortcomings before God. As John Wesley observed, *"Let every season, either of public or private fasting, be a season of exercising all those holy affections which are implied in a broken and contrite heart. Let it be a season of devout mourning, of godly sorrow for sin. . ."* It is this kind of godly mourning that is followed by *"the oil of gladness instead of mourning, the mantle of praise instead of fainting. So they will be called oaks of righteousness, the planting of the Lord, that He may be glorified"* (Isaiah 61:3).

4. They Fasted As A Sign of Repentance For Their Sin. Fasting, when combined with humility, confession, and mourning over our sin, is a true indication of genuine repentance. No where is this more clearly seen than in the example of Jonah and the Ninevites. In Jonah 3:5, in response to the preaching of the prophet, "the people of Nineveh believed in God; and they called a fast and put on sackcloth from the greatest to the least of them."Their action of fasting was matched with an attitude of repentance, *"let men call on God earnestly that each may turn from his wicked way and from the violence which is in his hands"* (Jonah 3:8). God

Preparing For A Spiritual Outpouring

graciously acknowledged the fasting of the Ninevites as an indication of genuine repentance, *"When God saw their deeds, that they turned from their wicked way, then God relented concerning the calamity which He had declared He would bring upon them. And He did not do it"* (Jonah 3:10).

Conclusion: The trouble with a "season" is that it is not a one-time event. You can't hold a "repentance" event, go through the motions for an hour and then declare victory and go home. I believe God is calling His church into a "season" of repentance. How long will it last? Until God "shows up" and lets us know that He has heard us, and that requires discipline and commitment. As we begin to fast, pray, confess and repent over the sins we know about, God may very well intervene and begin to show us the sins we DON'T know about that have been hindering His working. It's always the "little foxes" which spoil the vineyard (or as I recently told someone, "It's the things you don't remember that will kill you").

I can't speak for everyone on this list. You're "on your own." But I hope the things I've share "ring true." As for myself, I have decided to set aside the next 6 weeks (from now until Thanksgiving) as a period or season of personal fasting and repentance, because that's the part of God's season of dealing with us that I think we are now in, and I believe that it is absolutely imperative to take positive steps to embrace that season. So, what's my "church growth plan" for "mega-church growth" in house church? To fast, to pray, to repent and to ask God's forgiveness for being the obstacle in His Church that holds back what it is He wants to do. If I'm wrong, well, like I observed earlier, humility, contrition, brokenness and repentance are always a good thing with God.

He is coming. Are we ready? Is your House Church a channel through which He can flow?

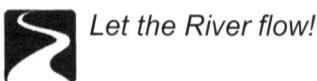 *Let the River flow!*

Transformation, Baseball and an Evening With George Otis, Jr. **3**

First Published August 31, 2005

This past weekend George Otis, Jr. ("Transformations") spoke at a local high school to a gathering sponsored by some 25 area churches. Some 300+ people showed up for the event. As the evening began I couldn't help but wonder *"Can anything good come out of Nazareth?"* The pre-printed program (*"Tri-County Transformation Rally Order of Service"*) announced the box-plan for the evening. An impromptu "Pastors Choir" would perform the "Call to Worship," followed by the required "Greeting and Opening Prayer" by one of the sponsoring Pastors. Eight songs later (4 "Songs of Worship" and 4 "Songs of Praise") George Otis would speak briefly (to whet our appetite), an offering would be taken, and then George would return and talk some more.

As the program began I realized that I had been "out of the box" a looooooooooog time. I felt my heart sinking with the idea that another box-program was underway, the exit was too far away to reach without being conspicuous, and, as Dante warned about situations like this, I should simply abandon all hope.

And then it happened. George Otis began speaking. Soon he was telling a story about a transformation rally in Cape Town, South Africa where he was to be the guest speaker. Everything was moving along religiously well according to the rally's program (complete with printed prayers), and George was bored to the point of insensibility. Finally, one of the Cape Town Pastors approached the master of Ceremonies and said, *"We need to take a risk."* As I listened, a light came on (yep, my lights aren't always on, but fortunately they do still work . . . occasionally). *"George Otis, you sly dog,"* I heard myself thinking, *"You aren't talking about a transformation rally in South Africa ! You're pulling a 'Jesus maneuver' on us, telling a story about someone else that's really making a point about US!"* I turned to my wife and said with a grin, *"He's talking about us; he's describing this meeting!"*

Preparing For A Spiritual Outpouring

Suddenly, I was awake, no longer bored, and contrary to Dante, I even felt hope rising up. Suddenly it was a new ball game, and I had just heard the crack of the bat announcing that a real game was underway. *"This could be good,"* I thought. Soon I was even taking notes. More stories (no, I'm not going to finish the South Africa story, but it was good - all about risky prayers and incredible answers!). Next, George related his perceptions of transformation rallies in Colombia and Africa. The difference between the two rallies, he observed, was the difference between a rally in Colombia to celebrate the transformation which God had brought about and a rally in Africa (no, I can't remember where) to plead with God for a coming transformation. Then, like a major league pitcher, he released a fastball right over the plate. We in America want to sing about and celebrate spiritual victories and an intimate relationship with God which belong to someone else, but which are not our experience or our reality. We need to pay the price of prayer, fasting and repentance to achieve our own victories, rather than celebrating the victories of other people in other places (what I call "vicarious revival"). *"Yes!"* I cried in my spirit. Another crack of the bat and this game was now well underway.

The meeting had now taken on a distinctively different tone, and I was fully engaged. *"Way to go, George!"* I thought to myself as he raised the bar, not of expectations but of divine demands. And he wasn't done yet. Most of our talk about revival in the Western church, he observed, is based upon our imaginations, because we have no memories (of actual revival). *"Exactly,"* I thought to myself. When I have compared my own studies in the history of revival to the "revival chatter" I hear today, I sense a profound disconnect, like of group of single college students discussing what marriage will be like. Memories of a good marriage are better (and more real) than single-hood imaginations about it. We need to ask God to replace our imaginations with memories. *"You're turning this meeting into an interesting ball game, George,"* I mused.

But there was more. Another pitch, the crack of the bat and we were suddenly in Isaiah 62: 6-7, *"On your walls, O Jerusalem,*

Chapter 3 - Transformation

I have appointed watchmen; all day and all night they will never keep silent. You who remind the Lord, take no rest for yourselves; and give Him no rest until He establishes and makes Jerusalem a praise in the earth." George observed that we in the Western church are the caboose (i.e., last car) on this transformation/revival train. Why? Because we are unwilling to interrupt our comfortable schedule and lifestyle in order to pursue it (I'm skipping over great illustrations, like God as the butler who serves us up a revival on our comfortable terms). Where is the dedicated ceaseless outcry for God's visitation? Why are we resting when we should be ceaselessly praying & fasting, giving God no rest until He answers?

Wow, another base hit into an unguarded centerfield. The game was now intense. Bases were loaded. The opposing team was getting trounced. The air in the room was hot and thick (literally), but the game wasn't over yet. More stories about God's Presence transforming various places in the world. Too many to relate here. Then came the wind-up and the "John Eldridge" question nobody expected . . . or wanted: *"Why do you want God to come and visit you? Who are you summoning, a fix-it handyman, or a lover?"* And there it was. A fast ball over the center of the plate and the crack of God's bat as the ball found the sweet spot of the evening. A bottom of the 9th, bases loaded, grand slam into the 3rd tier. This game was over. He had drilled the heart of the issue and exposed the bankrupt core of most of our revival & transformation rhetoric. Our view of revival and community transformation is essentially a vision of God coming as a divine "fix-it guy" who will conveniently fix all of the problems which we have created by our disobedience, fix and bless our existing paradigms ("something should happen, but nothing should change"), fix, clean up and transform our community, require little or nothing of us (none of this "negative" personal repentance business), and even leave us a blessing and gifts behind Him when he leaves! Who wouldn't want that?! But God wants to be our lover, not our repairman. Lovers want to be wooed, not proclaimed, ordered around or taken for granted. *"Who is this that grows like the dawn, as beautiful as the full moon, as pure as the sun, as awesome as an army with banners?"* (Song of Songs 6:10). It is the jealous bridegroom coming to woo his bride. What will he do if all he finds is a self-absorbed mistress who desires nothing more than a handyman who will repair the broken toilet seat?

I honestly don't know if George said anything after that moment. By this time my hair was on fire and I wasn't really aware of much else. He had been speaking for over an hour, and according to the program it was time for the long-delayed offering. Having just been confronted with a choice between Jesus as my handyman or as the lover of my soul, I was now confronted with the offering bucket. It was like taking a commercial break for spicy buffalo wings in the middle of watching "The Passion of The Christ." You could tell that many others felt the same way as there was an uneasiness in the room. I turned to my wife and observed, *"They need to cancel the offering or push it to the end and just move on quickly, but I'll bet you they can't bring themselves to do that."* Sure enough, a divine moment was interrupted (awkwardly and clumsily) with a commercial interlude. Following the interruption George Otis introduced a video promo for an upcoming video, "An Unconventional War," about the civil war in Uganda . It was good and powerful, but the highlight of the evening had already been achieved and had moved on. The evening closed with the mandatory altar call for those wanting to profess Christ and a line of area pastors waiting to receive them. *"They still aren't getting it,"* my wife opined (I've taught her all my bad habits . . . I'm so proud!).

As I reflected on the events of the evening I realized that God had spoken powerfully about what's to come and what we should be doing to prepare. The pastors who sponsored this event are good, dedicated and hard working people, many of whom have a genuine heart to see God do a new thing and move in fresh power. But true to our nature, we all tend to interpret the next move of God through the lenses of our existing paradigm, which generally reflects values left over from some previous move of God. So, when we hear that God is going to do a "new thing" (i.e., transformation, revival, etc.) we tend to interpret that to mean *"Oh, God's going to give us an upgrade."* But in reality, it means that God is going to shake us to our core, re-dig and re-build our foundations, and probably demolish several floors of our existing paradigm, assuming that He allows us to keep it at all.

As my wife and I left the meeting, I heard the pastor/MC instructing the audience on how to respond to what they had heard this evening, admonishing them to stay under the authority of their pastors because *"we don't need any loose cannons running around out there."* Oh, really? Guess again. I believe the one thing God DOES want in this season is a generation of believers whose hair has been set on fire with holy flame and who are determined not to allow anyone, clergy or otherwise, to put it out. Do you know what we call a person whose hair is on fire? A "hothead"! Just another name for . . . a loose cannon.

He is coming. Are we ready? Is your House Church a channel through which He can flow?

 Let the River flow!

Preparing For A Spiritual Outpouring

Intimacy, Authenticity, Spiritual Power & The Prayers of John Knox

4

First Published February 1, 2006

"Annie's a quiet girl, but she's deep. At least I hope she's deep. Otherwise, she's wasting a lot of time being quiet."

I grew up in a jewelry store. Well, almost. My father was a jeweler (and my mother a school teacher) all of my growing up life. I and my family spent many hours in dad's jewelry store helping out during the holiday seasons. And so I learned something about jewelry gold. I learned that there is a difference between a piece of jewelry that is 18 or 24 karat gold, and one that is simply 10 karat gold plate. If you have ever purchased gold plated jewelry then you know the disappointment that inevitably comes when the abrasiveness of life scratches the plating off and reveals the truth of what lies beneath. But 24 karat gold, on the other hand, is different. Regardless of how deep you scratch, it remains the same. It is "authentic," the same all the way through. Gold plated jewelry lacks authenticity, pretending to be something it really isn't.

Welcome to house church, and the challenge of genuine *ekklesia*, where God calls us into genuine intimacy with Himself and genuine authenticity with one another. Unfortunately, much of the contemporary American church resembles "Annie" rather than Tozer (O.K., it's a great line from the movie *"Royal Wedding"* with Fred Astaire). We gather together and hope that our silence regarding the issue of our personal intimacy with God will be mistaken for depth (the "cover up" being aided by generous amounts of what I call "bible babble"). But we live in the constant fear that someone will accidentally scratch through our 10 karat gold plating and discover the base metal which lies just beneath the surface.

It's my suspicion (which I can't prove, but speculation is a time-honored theological tradition!) that one of the root problems among the house churches of Corinth was a lack of intimacy with God, which eventually resulted in a lack of authenticity with one another. Paul's task in his letters to Corinth was to restore his apostolic authority which had been challenged, to rebuke false teachings and the teachers who brought it, to correct their spiritual abuses (power without intimacy or authenticity), deal with issues of sin (particularly immorality) and to encourage the Corinthians onward to a greater depth of intimacy with God and greater authenticity with one another.

The challenge of house church today is really no different today than it was 2000 years ago. I have written previously that, in its essence, house church is the pursuit of God in the company of friends who are learning to dance with God and with one another. I would "parse" this a bit more by adding that house church is also both a personal and a corporate journey into greater intimacy with God, which He desires (over time) to result in greater authenticity with one another. If, in our personal and corporate house church life together, there is no growing intimacy or authenticity, we will slowly but eventually devolve into a gathering of superficial acquaintances who meet to offer silence in place of depth, and who live in fear that someone may accidentally scratch off our 10 karat gold plating and discover "the awful truth" that lies beneath.

In our house church network I teach something called "Maurice's Maxim # 1" which unequivocally states: *"Life is messy!"*. Let's face reality. Our lives are "authentic messes" which God is in the process of redeeming as we journey together, a company of friends pursuing intimacy with God and authenticity with one another. So, let's drop the "religious act," scrape off the 10 karat gold plating, admit the messiness of our lives, and move on together in our personal and corporate journey of redemption and learning to dance with God and with each other.

Spiritual Power, and . . .

The stakes are surprisingly high in this struggle for intimacy and authenticity, especially when it comes to the relationship

Chapter 4 - Intimacy, Authority & Spiritual Power

between intimacy, authenticity and spiritual power. There is much talk and chatter among Christians today about "spiritual power" and "anointing," but much of the conversation is among people whose vocabulary has far out-run their actual experience level. For the most part, we are using the vocabulary of the last significant move of God in the misplaced hope that our words about power will somehow be mistaken for power itself, just as we hope others will mistake our silence for depth, and just as Moses hoped Israel would mistake the veil for the glory.

I believe there is an inescapable yet precarious relationship between intimacy, authenticity and power. Intimacy with God and authenticity with one another are indeed our common calling and goal. So is walking in spiritual power. Paul admonished the Corinthian believers who had lost both intimacy and authenticity. Apparently, they also stood on the brink of losing their spiritual power: *"But I will come to you soon, if the Lord wills, and I shall find out, not the words of those who are arrogant, but their power. For the kingdom of God does not consist in words, but in power."* (1 Corinthians 4:19-20)

Paul understood (do we?) that without intimacy with God, spiritual power will devolve into arrogance; and without authenticity with one another, spiritual power will expose and intensify the contradictions of our character, eventually resulting in self-destruction. As Graham Cooke so rightly observes, without such intimacy and authenticity, each of us will destroy with our character what we build with our gift. In God's design, intimacy will yield to authenticity, authenticity will build character, and character will prevent spiritual power from destroying both the one who wields it and the church through which it flows. I believe that God wants an *ekklesia* which moves in His power, and which walks in intimacy with Himself and authenticity with one another. Such a Church, offering to others the opportunity to "touch and taste the powers of the Age to Come", is a living, breathing model of the Kingdom of God that our Post Modern culture will be unable to refute . . . or resist. And that leads me to . . . .

Preparing For A Spiritual Outpouring

The Prayers of John Knox

Bear with me as I relate the story we all know so well. . . .

While others slept, he rose to pray . It was not the first time he had risen in the early morning hours to pray , nor would it be his last. The birth of a Church and the future of a nation demanded nothing less. So with only the stars and the angels as his witnesses, he wrestled with God over the future of his beloved but troubled nation. One of the sources of his nation's problems, Mary Queen of Scotland , had once remarked that she feared the prayers of this man more than she feared all the armies of Europe . If she could have witnessed his intercessions this night, her worst fears would have been confirmed, for here, alone beneath the stars, was a man who knew how to wrestle with God . . . and prevail.

"Great God," cried John Knox, "Give me Scotland , or I shall die."

The mantle of intercession that rested upon John Knox would one day be picked up and carried by his associate and son-in-law, John Welch, who would marry Knox's daughter, Elizabeth. Welch became widely known for his personal commitment to fasting and prayer, and for the significant amount of time he spent in personal prayer, often as much as eight hours a day. He also became known for tremendous spiritual power which seemed the outward result of his fervent intercessions. On more than one occasion his wife, Elizabeth, would awaken to an empty bed and find her husband praying alone in the cold night air of their garden, praying "with great force & fervency, mixed and accompanied with floods of tears," crying out, "Lord, wilt Thou not grant me Scotland?" She would remember the times she had heard her father, John Knox, pray with a similar burden on his heart, *"Great God, give me Scotland , or I shall die."* And how many times had she heard her husband wonder aloud how a Christian could lie in bed all night never rising to watch and pray .

Chapter 4 - Intimacy, Authority & Spiritual Power

Such are the wrestlings and intercessions of those whom God has used over the centuries, and continues to use today, to bring revival and to change the course of nations and of history. Throughout the history of His people, whenever God has intended to move in great spiritual power, He has always raised up people to carry the burden of prayer, fasting and intercession for what He intended to do. Such intercessors have always been the secret heralds of a coming visitation.

But have you ever asked yourself how we came to know that John Knox ever prayed such a prayer? We know about his prayer life . . . from his daughter, Elizabeth. Unlike so many people today, John Knox didn't pray this prayer in public - you know, the opening prayer at the General Assembly meeting. We know he prayed such a prayer in private early morning hours because that's when his family (those closest to us, and the hardest to impress) found him weeping and praying alone in the cold morning air.

Are You Fully Invested?

Along with prophesying a coming revival, praying a "John Knox prayer" has become somewhat of a cottage industry in certain quarters of the church today, sort of an ecclesiastical "right of passage" to prove one's "bona fides," if you will. I've done it too, so don't get me wrong. But only recently have I been brutally confronted with the full import of John Knox's prayer, what it truly meant to him, and what it truly means for those who would pray such a prayer today. It has changed the way I think, and the way I pray. I suspect that Knox's prayer is most often understood and explained as the bold prayer of a man who sought to achieve great things for God (I've certainly heard it interpreted that way). I now believe that interpretation to be 180-degrees wrong. I now genuinely and fervently believe it to be the prayer of a broken man who had found intimacy with God, was walking in authenticity with others (beginning with his own family who gave us this account of his private prayer life) and who was so "fully invested" in his prayers for the Kingdom of God that he would rather die than fail.

Preparing For A Spiritual Outpouring

What do I mean by "fully invested"? Like Hernando Cortez, who burned his boats when arriving in the New World (thereby eliminating "failing and going home" as an option), John Knox staked everything - his ministry, his reputation, the future of the Church of Scotland, and the future of his nation - on whether or not the God whom he intimately knew and with whom he authentically walked would answer his prayers, send revival and redeem his nation. John Knox wasn't afraid to die; rather, he was afraid to fail. And fear of failure gives birth to prayers of broken desperation which resonate through the hallways of heaven with cries of *"God take my life, but do not fail me."*

May I ask you a question? What's at risk in your prayers for spiritual out-pouring, revival and house church? How fully invested are you in your prayers for the Kingdom of God? Should God choose not to answer your "John Knox prayer," what do you stand to lose? Will life continue on more-or-less as normal? Will your "day job" continue on? Will your pension or 401(k) survive intact? Will the church or ministry continue on regardless, including booming internet sales of the wonderful message you preached on "God, give me Scotland , or I die"? If the answers to such questions are even a qualified "yes," then I question whether we have truly prayed the type of "fully invested" prayers of a John Knox, who preferred death over failure.

If You Could Do Something Else . . .

I'm going to surprise and potentially irritate some of you (what can I say, it's a gift!), so let me preface my comments with a story. In his book "Lectures To My Students," 19th Century English evangelist Charles Haddon Spurgeon used to tell his ministerial students in Spurgeon's College, *"If you can do anything else, other than be a pastor, do it! But if your spirit will not allow you to do anything else but be a pastor, then perhaps God is calling you to the ministry."* (Maurice's paraphrase).

I want to offer a similar exhortation to those of us aspiring to leadership in the house church movement in this unfolding season. If you could be content somewhere else, then that is probably where you should be. God is preparing to pour out the River of Ezekiel 47 in power and blessing the likes of which our generation has never experienced, and yes, it will flow through house churches. It will take us to a level of intimacy in God's Presence that few (if any) of us have ever known. Our experience may finally catch up with our vocabulary! It will also force us into an authentic _koinonia_ with one another that will be deep, rewarding, painful and biblical. It will release unprecedented spiritual power that will push and test our character to the breaking point . . . and beyond. And for this season God is calling out and raising up a generation of leaders who, like Elisha called from behind the plow, are willing to risk EVERYTHING, and who are so fully invested in what God wants to do by way of spiritual outpouring, transformation and revival through house churches that they would rather face death than failure. In this coming move of God's Spirit, many aspiring leaders will be touched by it, but few will be willing to take the risk and pay the price for truly entering in.

Are you one of them? He is coming. Are we ready? Is your House Church a channel through which He can flow?

 Let the River flow!

Preparing For A Spiritual Outpouring

"And Then They Repented"
An Examination of Zechariah 1:1-6
First Published February 23, 2006

5

"In the eighth month of the second year of Darius, the word of the Lord came to Zechariah the prophet, the son of Berechiah, the son of Iddo saying, 'The Lord was very angry with your fathers. Therefore say to them, 'Thus says the Lord of hosts, 'Return to Me,' declares the Lord of hosts, 'that I may return to you,' says the Lord of hosts. 'Do not be like your fathers, to whom the former prophets proclaimed, saying, 'Thus says the Lord of hosts, 'Return now from your evil ways and from your evil deeds.' But they did not listen or give heed to Me,' declares the Lord. 'Your fathers, where are they? And the prophets, do they live forever? 'But did not My words and My statutes, which I commanded My servants the prophets, overtake your fathers? Then they repented and said, 'As the Lord of hosts purposed to do to us in accordance with our ways and our deeds, so He has dealt with us.'" (Zechariah 1:1-6)

A couple of newsletters ago I made the observation that there are two ways to do the will of God. We can do the will of God voluntarily (what I call "the easy way"), or we can do the will of God involuntarily (what I call "the hard way"). The people of Zechariah's day had chosen to do God's will involuntarily (yep, the hard way), and therein lies a story.

Our story actually begins some 70 years earlier, prior to the Babylonian captivity. Josiah reigned as King over the Southern Kingdom of Judah (think Jerusalem & its suburbs) and the prophet Jeremiah ministered God's word. Josiah was a good King who led the nation through a period of revival and reformation. But it was a river wide and shallow. The hearts of the people remained essentially unchanged, and God (through His prophet) called the people to turn away from their spiritual adultery and to return to Him. He called them to repent. Repentance, both personal and corporate, stands out as one of the great and recurring themes of the book of Jeremiah (The Hebrew word for repent occurs some 112 times in Jeremiah).

Preparing For A Spiritual Outpouring

Judgment was coming, God declared, but there was still time to repent.

But it was not to be. The false prophets of peace and prosperity, of which there were at least as many then as today, found a receptive and willing audience. Their fifteen minutes of fame coincided with Judah's last fifteen minutes before disaster. Politicians with too much to lose, priests who should have known better and people who were comfortable in their spiritual adulteries, all turned a deaf ear to God's call of repentance and took their anger out on Jeremiah. The few remaining years of national existence quickly clicked by, the judgment of God fell and the Kingdom of Judah was carried away to Babylon and captivity, just as God - through Jeremiah - had promised.

Now, fast forward 70 years. The Babylonian captivity has ended and the people of God are once again returning to Jerusalem. Zechariah (along with his contemporary, Haggai) is ministering to the returnees and he opens his ministry with a spiritual history lesson (always a crowd pleaser!), which we find in Zechariah 1:1-6. Whether or not Zechariah meant to offer five points and a punchline, I'll never know. But it works for me, so here goes. I believe Zechariah wanted the people of Jerusalem to grasp five important historical/spiritual truths:

1. First, Zechariah wanted them to understand God's anger toward their fathers for their sin and disobedience. "The Lord was very angry with your fathers." The Babylonian Captivity hadn't been an accident of history, or the result of Judah's military ineptitude before a greatly superior enemy. It had been their God's sovereign act of judgment and punishment for their unrepented sin; the express consequence of both their actions and inactions. They had sown the wind, and had reaped the whirlwind, just as God had promised so many years before.

2. Second, he wanted to remind them of God's original command to their fathers to repent. *"Therefore say to them, 'Thus says the Lord of hosts, 'Return to Me,' declares the Lord*

Chapter 5 - And Then They Repented

of hosts, 'that I may return to you,' says the Lord of hosts." In a mere word and a moment's time Zechariah reminded them of Jeremiah's ministry to their fathers. There were probably old men in Zechariah's audience who, as children in Jerusalem, had personally heard Jeremiah deliver God's message of pending judgment and personal repentance (the Hebrew word translated "return" in Zechariah is also Jeremiah's favorite Hebrew word for "repent"). Old men heard old words with old ears, but with new understanding, as did their children.

3. Third, Zechariah wanted to pass along God's fresh admonishment to His people. *"Do not be like your fathers, to whom the former prophets proclaimed, saying, 'Thus says the Lord of hosts, 'Return now from your evil ways and from your evil deeds.' But they did not listen or give heed to Me,' declares the Lord."* Zechariah was building a lesson here by translating a past disaster of disobedience into a present opportunity for obedience and blessing. Learn from the past. Don't be like your fathers, who heard the word of repentance but "did not listen or give heed." The unspoken question hanging in the air was, "Would the new generation of the children learn from the experience of their fathers?" Only time would tell.

4. Fourth, he wanted them to understand God's persistence. *"Your fathers, where are they? And the prophets, do they live forever? 'But did not My words and My statutes, which I commanded My servants the prophets, overtake your fathers?"* To put this in contemporary terms, the people of God had been "overtaken" by "the hound of heaven," Who pursues the object of His eternal desire with a relentless love. The word of repentance proclaimed by Jeremiah had not been received, but neither had it "gone away." When God calls a man or a people to repent, the call of God will always outlast the man, or the people. God's call of repentance to the fathers had been rejected, yet it remained. The people thought their refusal was the "last word." But God's word is always the last word. God's word "overtook" the fathers. When did that take place? In the Babylonian Captivity. God's word of repentance had not evaporated into the spiritual ether. Rather it had moved from the "easy" stage (when they could have repented rather easily & voluntarily) into the "hard" stage, when their repentance would come harder (even "involuntarily") and at a much higher price. The word of repentance which had been delivered and rejected during days of heady arrogance and seemingly clear skies had "overtaken" them in dark and stormy days of disaster, calamity and captivity.

5. Fifth, Zechariah wanted them to grasp God's unfailing purpose, namely, to bring His people to renewed repentance and faith. Then they repented and said, *'As the Lord of hosts purposed to do to us in accordance with our ways and our deeds, so He has dealt with us.'* It must have been an uncomfortable dawning, a bitter realization that God had indeed accomplished His purpose which He had declared so many years before. At some unspecified point during the Babylonian Captivity the fathers had repented and acknowledged that everything which had happened to them was simply the deserved consequences of God dealing with them *"in accordance with our ways and our deeds."* That had to hurt, and it certainly left a mark.

Conclusion: Zechariah's point (as I understand it) in this spiritual history lesson was really quite simple: The fathers who had heard God's call to repentance, experienced God's judgment and eventually repented, had also discovered that there are two ways to do the will of God: voluntarily (that would be the easy way) or involuntarily (that would be the hard way). Their fathers could have repented 70 years earlier, and like all such missed opportunities, we can only guess what the results of that repentance might have been. But they eventually did repent, and that is the prolonged point of this story.

Repentance Then and Now

Some things haven't really changed in 2,500 years. Repentance remains an unpopular message, even today, whether among the seeker-friendly masses who want their best life now (*sans* repentance), or among complacent

Chapter 5 - And Then They Repented

contemporary Christians who think that repentance is something reserved for "really bad people": pedophiles, chainsaw murders or worse . . . such as politicians from the other party.

As a result, in the contemporary church repentance has, for the most part, suffered twin fates. On the one hand, it has itself been purposely driven out of seeker friendly churches like an unwelcome demon. After all, to call men (and women) to repent and shun those deeds of the flesh which they love and to embrace those godly virtues which our old un-repentant nature despises is, well, uncool. Not exactly a congregation builder, according to the best church growth manuals. On the other hand, repentance has suffered the ignominious fate of respectability and "Christian-political-correctness" in the house of those who should have been its subjects. Aspiring leaders who have never met and do not know (much less sinned against) their stage counterparts to whom they are assigned and scheduled to repent, shed pseudo-tears as they lead pseudo-penitents through the formalized steps of pseudo-repentance in the hope that the pseudo-deities of their imagination will be somehow pleased with their pseudo-offerings. To witness and reflect on such performances is to suddenly realize that the "mistake" of God's people in Jeremiah's day was not their failure to repent of their spiritual adultery and idolatry. Rather, their real "mistake" was their failure to find a Canaanite (or a Phoenician, since they are related) and to formally repent to them and ask forgiveness for their Jewish ancestors having slaughtered their Phoenician ancestors and stealing their land. This, of course could have opened the door to a virtually limitless cottage industry, since the same procedure would need to be engaged in on behalf of the Hivites, the Hittites, the Perizzites, the Girgshites, the Kenites, the Jebusites, the Amorites and "every-other-ite" between Egypt and Mesopotamia. The potential for repentance events, books, CDs and DVDs would have been endless . . . but, alas, I digress . . . .

Preparing For A Spiritual Outpouring

Pseudo-Repentance In Jeremiah's Day

Lest you think I am "over-reaching" my point, allow me to point out that such formalized but empty spiritual exercises are not new. They were taking place in Jeremiah's day, too. How do I know that? Because he says so, *"So the Lord said to me, 'Do not pray for the welfare of this people. When they fast, I am not going to listen to their cry; and when they offer burnt offering and grain offering, I am not going to accept them. Rather I am going to make an end of them by the sword, famine and pestilence."* (Jeremiah 14:11-12) Biblical fasting is a God-appointed means of expressing personal repentance, as well as a personal act of sacrificial worship (i.e., worship which costs us something). But the people of Jeremiah's day had reached a point of "religiousness" in which they went through the motions without the heart or the spirit. They outwardly fasted - went through the religious motions - but did not repent nor worship. And to fast without genuinely repenting is like praying without ever talking to God. Don't bother, because God isn't in it. For this reason alone it is not surprising that God specifically instructed Jeremiah (15:19-21) to practice a lifestyle of genuine personal repentance before Him. Only then would God restore him, cause him to stand before Him, teach him to "extract the precious from the worthless" (i.e., exercise discernment) and truly become "My spokesperson." Such a man (or woman) living such an authentic lifestyle of genuine humility and repentance toward God would indeed become "a fortified wall of bronze" in an age of spiritual and moral mud huts.

Repentance And House Church

My view of repentance is the same as my view of sin: I prefer the real thing over any imitation or substitute. I find it difficult, to the point of incredulity, to believe that we have so few personal, real and immediate sins in need of confession and repentance that we must dig up dead ancestors and repent for them. Any good Mormon must be thoroughly confused at this point. They baptize for their dead ancestors (hence, their profound interest

Chapter 5 - And Then They Repented

in genealogy). We merely repent for ours. I doubt a good Mormon understands the theological difference . . . and I doubt that most good evangelicals could begin to explain it to them.

O.K., If I haven't gored your sacred cow yet, please send me a note and I'll try to fit it into next week's letter. In the mean time please bear with me as I bring this lesson home (literally) to house church.

First, as I have stated before on numerous occasions, I believe that the River of God's Spirit, the River of Ezekiel 47, is preparing to flow in great spiritual power and blessing not seen in our generation. We will all be surprised at what God is about to do. And it is my firm conviction that God is raising up the house church movement as one of the new channels through which His River will flow to this generation. And repentance is God's way of keeping His channels clean so that His River can flow unimpeded. Do you want more of God in your personal life and the life of your house church? Do you want more of His Spirit, His Presence, His Intimacy. Then repent of those things, however great or however small, which grieve His Spirit, quench His Presence and prevent His intimacy.

Second, there is much talk today about generational curses as if Christians have suddenly discovered some new spiritual truth. They haven't. Some thirty years ago Dr. Kurt Koch (Th.D.) wrote a book entitled Christian Counseling and Occultism (Kregel Publications, 1972) in which he documented clinical counseling cases of individuals suffering from a wide variety of disorders, the origins of which could be directly traced back to family (parents or grand parents) who were involved with the occult. The solution? Recognition, confession and repentance. Want to break generational curses (real ones, as opposed to the numerous fake ones being talked about today)? Spend quality time with God fasting, praying, confessing the sins and strongholds in your own life and REPENTING of them. You don't need a genealogy chart documenting your family sins all the way back to the tribe of Reuben (true story, no time). You will be amazed at what God can do with a heart that seeks him

Preparing For A Spiritual Outpouring

in simple prayer, fasting and genuine repentance.

Third, it was John Donne (1572-1631), the English poet and pastor who wrote,

"No man is an island, entire of itself; every man is a piece of the continent, a part of the main; if a clod be washed away by the sea, Europe is the less, as well as if a promontory were, as well as if a manor of thy friends or of thine own were; any man's death diminishes me, because I am involved in mankind; and therefore never send to know for whom the bell tolls; it tolls for thee."

Yep, I know. I could have quoted Paul from 1 Corinthians 12 about the various parts of the body being important and connected, but you probably would have recognized the quote and told yourself, "Yeah, yeah, I've heard all that" (familiarity really does breed contempt!). So I decided to let John Donne carry the water for me on this one. Do you get his point? I have a vested interest in your repentance . . . and you have a vested interest in mine. Why? Because as believers we share a common life in the body of Christ (and, for our purposes here, in the house church movement), and hence, we share a common fate as Jesus chastens, disciplines and cleanses His Church.

When the Holy Spirit begins to "toll the bell" of repentance in the Church, do not *"send to know for whom the bell tolls; it tolls for thee."*

He is coming. Are we ready? Is your House Church a channel through which He can flow?

 Let the River flow!

42

When The Holy Spirit Comes Via Inter Library Loan

First Published April 6, 2006

The Hem of His Garment

It isn't every day that the Holy Spirit arrives via Inter-Library Loan, but that's basically what happened this week. And therein lies a story. I have an almost unquenchable thirst for the history of God's dealings which we refer to as "revival". I don't particularly care for most of the recently penned works about revival, as so many of them are not so much histories as polemics which use snippets from the history of revival to promote a particular "revival agenda." For this reason I am always "on the hunt" for original material by people who were personally present when God "rent the heavens and came down." I scour the footnotes of books and articles in search of a thread I can grab and begin pulling in the hope of finding one that will lead me to the hem of a garment worn by "one who was there." Such a thread, found in the footnote of an article by veteran Presbyterian missionary Samuel Moffett, led me to the garment of William Newton Blair.

In 1904 a worldwide outpouring began, starting in the tiny country of Wales. Beginning as a burning coal fresh from God's altar under the ministry of pastor Joseph Jenkins (New Quay Church in Cardiganshire, Wales) in February of 1904, it became a spreading flame in the itinerant ministry of evangelist Seth Joshua, until the fall of 1904 when it burst into an uncontrollable wildfire led and fanned by a 26 year old former coal miner and Bible school student named Evan Roberts. The River of Ezekiel 47 was poured out in power the likes of which has seldom been seen or experienced among God's people. Beginning in Wales it flowed east, west, north and south, making a brief stop at an abandoned livery stable turned church on Azusa Street in Los Angeles in 1906, and finally ending up among Presbyterian Missionaries (we Presbyterians are slow, but we do catch on!) in Korea, meeting with their congregations for a week of Bible school during the first week of January, 1907.

Preparing For A Spiritual Outpouring

Korea 1907

It is there, in the Central Presbyterian Church in Pyengyang, Korea that we find William Newton Blair. Arriving in Korea in 1901, the Blair's would spend the next 45 years as missionaries to Korea. In the winter of 1907, some 1,500 Korean men gathered in the Central Church in Pyengyang for their annual Presbyterian Men's Bible study class. Only a couple of months earlier Dr. Howard Agnew Johnson had visited the church and told of how the spreading worldwide awakening had reached India with great blessing. Daily prayer meetings had begun among the Korean believers during the Christmas holiday season. The week of Bible classes began on January 2 and proceeded uneventfully, but with a growing sense of anticipation that God was at work. On Saturday evening, at the end of the first week, they began a series of pre-planned evening meetings as part of the Bible Class. Saturday night passed uneventfully. *"Nothing unusual happened,"* said Blair, *"We were not looking for anything unusual. Only a hushed, upturned sea of solemn faces and eagerness to lead in prayer showed how the Spirit was working."* According to Blair, *"We went home that night confident that our prayers were being answered. Sunday night we had a strange experience. The church was crowded, but something seemed to block everything. After the sermon a few formal prayers were offered and we went home weary as from a physical contest, conscious that the adversary was present, apparently victorious."*

Little did they (or could they) anticipate what was about to unfold. What follows, *"The Korean Pentecost,"* is William Newton Blair's account in his own words.

"The Korean Pentecost"
(From Gold In Korea, by William Newton Blair)

Monday noon, we missionaries met and cried out to God in earnest. We were bound in spirit and refused to let God go until He blessed us. That night it was very different. Each felt as he entered the church that the room was full of God's presence.

Chapter 6 - When The Holy Spirit Comes

Not only missionaries, but Koreans testified to the same thing. I was present once in Wisconsin when the Spirit of God fell upon a congregation of lumbermen and every unbeliever in the room rose to ask for prayers. That night in Pyengyang, the same feeling came to me as I entered the room, a feeling of God's nearness impossible to describe.

After a short sermon, Dr. Lee took charge of the meeting and called for prayers. So many began praying that Dr. Lee said, 'If you want to pray like that, all pray,' and the whole audience began to pray out, all together. The effect was indescribable. Not confusion, but a vast harmony of sound and spirit, a mingling together of souls moved by an irresistible impulse to prayer. It sounded to me like the falling of many waters, an ocean of prayer beating against God's throne. It was not many, but one, born of one Spirit, lifted to one Father above. Just as on the Day of Pentecost they were all together in one place, of one accord praying, 'and suddenly there came from heaven the sound as of the rushing of a mighty wind, and it filled all the house where they were sitting.'

God is not always in the whirlwind, neither does He always speak in a still small voice. He came to us in Pyengyang that night with the sound of weeping. As the prayer continued a spirit of heaviness and sorrow came down upon the audience. Over on one side someone began to weep and in a moment the whole congregation was weeping.

Dr. Lee's account, written at the time of the revival, gives the history of that night better than any words written later, however carefully penned, can do. *"Man after man would rise, confess his sin, break down and weep, and then throw himself on the floor and beat the floor with his fists in perfect agony of conviction. My own cook tried to make a confession, broke down in the midst of it and cried to me across the room, 'Pastor, tell me, is there any hope for me, can I be forgiven, and then he threw himself to the floor and wept and wept, and almost screamed in agony. Sometimes after a confession, the whole audience would break out in audible prayer and the effect of that audience of hundreds of men praying together in audible prayer was something indescribable. Again, after another confession they would break out in uncontrollable weeping and we would all weep together, we couldn't help it. And so the meeting went on until two o'clock a.m., with confession and weeping and praying."*

Only a few missionaries were present Monday night. Tuesday morning, Dr. Lee and I went from house to house telling those who were absent about the meeting. That noon the whole foreign community assembled to render thanks to God.

I wish to describe that Tuesday night meeting in my own words because part of what happened concerned me personally. We were aware that bad feeling existed between several of our church officers, especially between a Mr. Kang and a Mr. Kim. Mr. Kang confessed his hatred for Mr. Kim on Monday night, but Mr. Kim was silent. At our noon prayer-meeting Tuesday several of us agreed to pray for Mr. Kim. I was especially interested because Mr. Kang was my assistant in the North Pyengyang Church and Mr. Kim, an elder in the Central Church and one of the officers in the Young Men's Association of which I was chairman. As the meeting progressed, I could see Mr. Kim sitting with the elders back of the pulpit with his head down. Bowing where I sat I asked God to help him and looking up I saw him coming forward.

Holding to the pulpit he made his confession. *'I have been guilty of fighting against God. An elder in the church, I have been guilty of hating not only Kang You-moon, but Pang Moksa.'* "Pang Moksa" was my Korean name. I never had a greater surprise in my life. To think that this man, my associate in the Men's Association, had been hating me without my knowing it. It seems that I had said something to him one day in the hurry of managing a school field day exercise which had given offense, and he had not been able to forgive me.

Turning to me he said, *'Can you forgive me? Can you pray for me?'* I stood up and began to pray, *"Aba-ge, Aba-ge," "Father,*

Chapter 6 - When The Holy Spirit Comes

Father," and got no further. It seemed as if the roof was lifted from the building and the Spirit of God came down in a mighty avalanche of power upon us. I fell at Kim's side and wept and prayed as I had never prayed before. My last glimpse of the audience is photographed indelibly on my brain. Some threw themselves full length on the floor, hundreds stood with arms outstretched towards heaven. Every man forgot every other. Each was face to face with God. I can hear yet that fearful sound of hundreds of men pleading with God for mercy.

As soon as we were able, we missionaries gathered at the platform and consulted. *'What shall we do? If we let them go on this way some will go crazy.'* Yet we dared not interfere. We had prayed to God for an outpouring of His Holy Spirit upon the people and it had come. Separating, we went down and tried to comfort the most distressed, pulling the agonized men to the floor and saying, *'Never mind, brother, if you have sinned God will forgive you. Wait and an opportunity will be given to speak.'*

Finally Dr. Lee started a hymn and quiet was restored during the singing. Then began a meeting the like of which I had never seen before, nor wish to see again unless in God's sight it is absolutely necessary. Every sin a human being can commit was publicly confessed that night. Pale and trembling with emotion, in agony of mind and body, guilty souls standing in the white light of that judgment, saw themselves as God saw them. Their sins rose up in all their vileness 'till shame and grief and self-loathing took complete possession. Pride was driven out; the face of man forgotten. Looking up to heaven, to Jesus whom they had betrayed, they smote themselves and cried out with bitter wailing, *"Lord, Lord, cast us not away forever."* Everything else was forgotten; nothing else mattered. The scorn of men, the penalty of the law, even death itself seemed of small consequence if only God forgave. We may have our theories of the desirability or undesirability of public confession of sin. I have had mine, but I know now that when the Spirit of God falls upon guilty souls there will be confession and no power on earth can stop it. **(End of Blair Account)**

Preparing For A Spiritual Outpouring

Dying To Our Agendas

As I sat at my desk reading this account of God's dealings with people not unlike you and me, I had a profound sense that the Holy Spirit was speaking. Suddenly and unconsciously I found myself thumbing through the opening pages of the book, examining the title page, the copyright page, the dedication page . . . and there I found it. Written in blue ink and in William Newton Blair's own hand was this dedication: *"To my beloved wife and partner in everything, Stella N. Blair, with deep affection and appreciation. William N. Blair."* Then a note in Korean, followed by "with my loving greetings - Pang Util Yang" (his Korean name). I suddenly realized that, compliments of the University of Oregon, Eugene, I was holding in my hands Blair's personal copy of his personal account of the day when "God rent the heavens and came down." Suddenly time and distance collapsed and disappeared as I heard the Spirit of God ask, *"Is this what you seek? Is this the outpouring you desire? Are you prepared to welcome me on my terms?"* I sat on my couch and wept the tears of one confronted with his own death, and yet strangely longing for it more than one would long for life. And the Holy Spirit visited me in my study, via Inter Library Loan.

There is much talk today about both revival and house church. Much of the revival talk that I have heard, and much of the activity I have seen, resembles men attempting to organize a parade complete with food, music & entertainment in the hope that God will show up and agree to lead it. I confess that there have been times that I, too, have engaged in the same behavior. But is that really God's heart? And is that really what we want God to do? Is that what we are praying and longing for in terms of "revival"? Or are we willing to invite God to "rend the heavens and come down" and to send the Holy Spirit on His terms, even if the price of such a visitation includes our own profound "death-to-self"? Parades are fun - death to self is not.

Revival, Structures & Values

And what does all of this have to do with house church? Bill

Chapter 6 - When The Holy Spirit Comes

Beckham, an internationally recognized leader in the cell church movement, makes a profound observation when he observes, *"You never change a structure until you change a value. We do not transplant systems and structures. We transplant values and life."* Amen! Much of what I have observed and experienced in our movement thus far, including the current rising interest in house church among traditional church practitioners, represents a "fiddling with the structure," an experimentation with methodology, rather than a genuine imbibing and incarnation of new values - new wine skins sans the requisite new wine. This cannot and will not last. Infatuation with the "novel" never does. When I look at the "house-to-house" church movement of Acts 2:41-47 I am reminded that it was the product of Acts 2:1-40 and the Pentecostal outpouring of the Holy Spirit that brought thousands to new-found faith in Christ (just as the exploding church of Korea over the past 100 years is nothing less than the product of that 1907 outpouring of the Holy Spirit). The new wine of Acts 2:1-40 produced the new wine skins of Acts 2:41-47. That's the way it works. Not the other way around. If we are not careful, "house church" will become little more than a new structure in search of a value, a wine skin in search of wine. And that would be disastrous.

But I believe that God has different plans. Like those Presbyterian missionaries and Korean believers of 1907, I believe we are standing on the eve of an outpouring of the River of Ezekiel 47 the like of which has not been seen or experienced in well over 100 years. And like those early believers of Acts Chapter 2, this is the "value" that will create, fill and guide our structure throughout this generation, and probably well into the next. But I believe that the Spirit of God would ask you the same question which He asked me (yep, via Inter Library Loan!): *"Is this what you seek? Is this the outpouring you desire? Are you prepared to welcome me on my terms?"* Are you? Are you prepared to embrace the profound "death-to-self" that it may (and probably will) require? Are you prepared for your house church to become a new channel through which the River of his Spirit can flow?

Preparing For A Spiritual Outpouring

When the "values" of our house church "structure" is examined by future generations, let it be said of us, *"They set their hearts to become a channel through which the River of God could flow . . . and He did."*

He is coming. Are we ready? Is your House Church a channel through which He can flow?

 Let the River flow!

A Couple of Bones To Pick With George Otis, Jr.

Most of you are probably aware of George Otis, Jr. and the Sentinel Group who have produced the "Transformation" videos over the past few years. The videos are wonderful encouragements about how God is working in transforming ways in various places around the world. Last summer I wrote an e-mail about my experience in a meeting where George Otis, Jr. was speaking outside of Spokane in Deer Park (see Chapter 3, page 21, *"Transformation, Baseball and an Evening With George Otis, Jr."*).

But I have two bones to pick with how the videos and the experiences of transformation around the world are currently being interpreted and even marketed. **First,** the videos are becoming a "vicarious revival experience" for the people & communities who watch them. George Otis himself addressed this issue when he spoke here in August, last year. Here is what I wrote about his treatment of this issue then: *"Next, George related his perceptions of transformation rallies in Colombia and Africa. The difference between the two rallies, he observed, was the difference between a rally in Colombia to celebrate the transformation which God had brought about and a rally in Africa (no, I can't remember where) to plead with God for a coming transformation. Then, like a good marksman, He released the arrow at his unsuspecting targets: We in America want to sing about and celebrate spiritual victories and an intimate relationship with God which belong to someone else, but which are not our experience or our reality. We need to pay the price of prayer, fasting and repentance to achieve our own victories, rather than celebrating the victories of other people in other places (what I call "vicarious revival")."* It is always easier to vicariously enter into someone else's experience of revival than it is to pay the price necessary to experience it for ourselves.

And this leads me to my **second** bone to pick, namely, the

Preparing For A Spiritual Outpouring

creation of a "one-size-fits-all" model of revival (i.e., God always works this way . . .). Think of this in terms of the letters of Christ to the seven churches of Asia. Here were seven different letters to seven very different churches, each letter dealing with issues unique to that particular church (but with general application to other churches in other times). But today, in our treatment of transformation and revival, its as though Jesus, writing to those same churches today, would write just one letter and say, *"Here, just circulate this letter among yourselves, 'cause you're all the same anyway"!* O, really? I don't think so. I think both scripture and history would argue otherwise.

Let me be more specific. One of the popular messages (or interpretations) that has come out of the videos concerns the idea of "unity" in the body as a necessary prelude to revival. The argument runs something like this. *"In such and such a place, the pastors all came together and prayed together and the result was revival. Therefore, we must have unity among the pastors, the churches and the body before we can experience revival here."* But what if "unity" was God's message to the church in that city for a special reason which is not necessarily transferable to your city (not that unity is bad, it simply isn't God's message for your city)? Look at what the history of revival says about the need for "unity" with respect to revival. During the Evangelical Awakening in England in the 1700s, the only unity among the Anglican Churches was their united resistance to both George Whitefield and John Wesley, both of whom were "shut out" of Anglican pulpits throughout England (despite being ordained Anglican priests) and were forced to resort to open-air preaching in fields and town squares. During the Second Great Awakening in America (1799-1811) there was both co-operation and dissension. Two of the leaders of the Second Great Awakening, the Reverends James McGready and Barton Stone, were charged with heresy by the Presbyterian Church for their participation in the revival (McGready "repented" while Stone left the Presbyterian Church). And during the Welsh Revival of 1904, Evan Roberts was viciously attacked in the press by leading members of his own denomination, the Calvinistic Methodists (the Reverend

Chapter 7 - A Couple of Bones To Pick

Peter Price being the most vocal).

So, is "unity" the "linchpin" for revival? Not necessarily. The New Testament speaks more of *homothumadon* - "one-mindedness" - than it does of unity, but I'll let you do that study for yourself. Much of our efforts at "unity" in the church are manifestations of what M. Scott Peck ("The Different Drum") calls "pseudocommunity." The real "linchpin" for revival in any given city probably has more to do with the besetting sins and spiritual strongholds of that city. Here in Spokane & Eastern Washington where I live and work, I have been deeply impressed over the past two years that the "linchpin" for revival in our area is not unity among believers, churches and organizations, but repentance for our sins, our failures and our disobedience of walking in spiritual strongholds that God despises. What are the spiritual strongholds that need to be the focus of that repentance? There are three which take prominence: 1) the spirit of religion -wanting and working to look outwardly religious; 2) the spirit of control - wanting to control people and how they live their spiritual lives, rather than loving them and equipping them for the work of the ministry; and 3) the spirit of mammon - wanting to control money, which becomes another form of controlling people in ministry. Acknowledgment, confession and repentance of these three spiritual strongholds, I believe, is the linchpin of widespread spiritual revival and transformation in our community.

He is coming. Are we ready? Is your House Church a channel through which He can flow?

 Let the River flow!

Preparing For A Spiritual Outpouring

And Then They Repented?
Reflections On Ted Haggard, Repentance & Revival
First Published November 6, 2006

8

Recent Events & Two Lessons

The Evangelical Christian community was dealt a body blow this past week by accusations leveled against Ted Haggard, President of the National Association of Evangelicals and Pastor of the 14,000 member New Life Church in Colorado, Springs. The accusations involved drug use and a homosexual tryst with a Denver male prostitute over a span of nearly 3 years. In a letter read to his former congregation on Sunday Pastor Haggard admitted: *"The fact is I am guilty of sexual immorality. And I take responsibility for the entire problem. I am a deceiver and a liar. There's a part of my life that is so repulsive and dark that I have been warring against it for all of my adult life,"* My suspicion (and my fear) is that there is probably more to this, and that the Evangelical community and the world at large will probably be subjected, compliments of a hyper-active media, to a form of Chinese water torture as additional details come dripping out. I can "hardly wait" to see what tabloid headlines appear at local supermarket news stands in the coming weeks. As a friend of mine might say to summarize, *"This is an ugly pig, and putting lipstick on it won't help"*.

I do not know Pastor Haggard at all, although I have friends and ministry associates who do and, up til now, have held him in very high regard. I cannot speak to his personal character or behavior. I must leave that to others. I ache and weep for his wife and family who must now walk with him through a valley of personal trial and humiliation that most of us cannot begin to fathom. I refuse to engage in personal recriminations and statements such as *"Well, he's reaping what he sowed"* or *"He's a hypocrite and he's getting what he deserves."* While there may be a grain of truth to such statements (we do, indeed, reap what we sow, and God does indeed hate hypocrisy), such statements miss two important truths. First,

55

Preparing For A Spiritual Outpouring

they miss the truth that the Church of Jesus is an "army" called upon to show mercy toward its "enemies" and compassion towards its wounded. Unfortunately, all too often we are the army which vilifies its "enemies" and shoots its own wounded. For my part, I plan to pray for Ted and for his beleaguered family who, in this night season of their lives, must feel like they are walking through the valley of the shadow of death. Been there. Have a tee-shirt. Nuff said. But there is a second truth that I fear we may miss in the midst of this messy fracas and media feeding frenzy, and it is a truth much larger than Ted Haggard. It's a truth about God's call upon His church at this time, and that's a three-year story I need to briefly unpack.

A Message of Repentance

Much of what I am about to BRIEFLY relate can be traced through back issues of this newsletter, so I will reference them as I go along, should you want to explore in more detail what I am about to relate in brief. Three years ago, beginning in October of 2003 (see Chapter 2, page 13) I began hearing from the Lord that He was calling His Church into a season of profound repentance in preparation for Revival. My sense of this calling grew in intensity to the point that I felt led to announce a season of prayer, fasting and repentance for revival among Churches in the greater Spokane area (see our newsletter for January 13, 2004 posted on our website). We prepared audio messages, radio programs, printed materials and more and sent some 200 packets to prominent local area churches encouraging them to participate. The response was, well, "tepid" at best ("tepid" sounds more generous than "non-existent"). Following this season I was asked by Paul Kaak (of Organic Greenhouses) if I thought this was a message for the larger Church in America. Not feeling called as a "prophet to the nations" I felt ill-equipped to answer that question. Over the year that followed I wondered if God's call to repentance had waned or if I had "mis-heard." Then, at a prayer conference sponsored by one of the pastors of the local Korean Presbyterian Church in Spokane in October of 2005, the Holy Spirit "surprised" me with a renewed call to the Church

Chapter 8 - And Then They Repented?

in Spokane to repent (yep, same response). I didn't fully understand what God was saying or doing by this renewed call until February when the Lord took me to Zechariah 1:1-6 and showed me the difference between "easy" repentance and "hard" repentance. He showed me that the Church had ignored and rejected His season of "easy" repentance and was now entering a season of "hard" repentance (see Chapter 5, page 35). Feeling that I had "done my duty" I tried over the next few months to set this message aside and concentrate on other things. But once God declares a season, He sees it through to the end, regardless of what we do . . . or don't do. I had been working on an extended treatment of repentance in the letters to the 7 churches of Asia in Revelation 2-3, but set the study aside this summer in the hope that my involvement was done. Right. Then, in September the Lord surprised me (again) with a strong sense that we were entering a season during which He would answer the "desperate prayers" of His people. What I didn't know then was how God planned to bring His church to a point of desperation - you see, it takes desperate people to pray desperate prayers. And that's where Ted Haggard enters in to what God is doing right now.

Repentance And God's Megaphone

C.S. Lewis said that pain is God's megaphone by which He gets the attention of a deaf world. The same "principle of pain" applies to a deaf Church. Just how "deaf" we are can often be measured by the level of pain God must inflict (or allow) in order to get our attention. For the past three years God has been vying for the attention of His Church in Spokane, calling it to seek Him in genuine repentance and humility. But His message has been hindered by a profound spiritual deafness masked by a pseudo-boldness which seeks to proclaim its way into revival while by-passing God's pathway - the "road-not-taken" which leads through the low-places of personal humility, confession of sin and repentance. I am only beginning to appreciate that this message is much larger than Spokane. It is God's call upon His greater Church in America, and His necessary precursor to genuine revival. The Holy Spirit

Preparing For A Spiritual Outpouring

simply will not fill dirty, un-repentant vessels. So is it any surprise that He is beginning to "wash the dishes"?

Several weeks ago my wife, Gale, heard a word during her devotions that *"things hidden in darkness are going to be revealed"*. A week ago, who could have imagined the events of the past week and the "dark" things which have come to light. I have literally had local Christian leaders tell me that they have nothing to repent of and don't see the need for this message. I hope the events of the past week have helped change that attitude. I hope so, but I'm not overly optimistic. But if not, more is coming. We are now in a season of "hard" repentance for the Church, during which delay will only intensify what unfolds. God is indeed preparing to answer the desperate prayers of desperate believers. And if need be, He will increase the level of our desperation by turning up the volume of His divine but painful megaphone until He overcomes our deafness and achieves a broken, contrite, humble and repentant people who have ears and can hear what the Spirit is saying to the church.

Several churches in Spokane are sponsoring a 24 Hour worship gathering at a local church. If I had a voice in the leadership of this event (which I don't), I would encourage, even insist, that the event not focus on "cheap worship." Cheap worship is worship which doesn't cost us anything. Most contemporary worship is "cheap" by this definition. There is no price tag attached other than the cost of time spent. Repentance, on the other hand, is "expensive" worship. It costs us something, things like our pride, our religious, pseudo-spiritual veneer, the confession of hidden sins, and more. But there is also a "cheap" form of repentance that must also be avoided as well. It is the "staged" repentance of Christian "political correctness." In "Cheap" repentance, aspiring leaders who have never met and do not know (much less sinned against) their stage counterparts to whom they are assigned and scheduled to repent, shed pseudo-tears as they lead pseudo-penitents through the formalized steps of pseudo-repentance in the hope that the pseudo-deities of their imagination will somehow be pleased with their

Chapter 8 - And Then They Repented?

pseudo-offerings. Can "representational" or "identificational" repentance be effective and meaningful? Yes, of course, but only when it is spontaneous, genuine and Holy Spirit driven. But not as an agenda item on the evening's program. Repentance is not a spectator sport to be performed by some and enjoyed by others. Confessing someone else's sin as if it were our own is far easier than asking God to reveal the secret sins and strongholds of our own heart. Jeremiah the prophet understood this dilemma when he declared: *"The heart is more deceitful than all else and is desperately sick; Who can understand it?"* Then came the divine answer: *"I, the LORD, search the heart, I test the mind, even to give to each man according to his ways, according to the results of his deeds."* In genuine repentance we submit the deceitfulness and sickness of our individual hearts to God who searches and tests all things, and Who reveals to us those things which we have hidden from men, from God . . . and even from ourselves.

Allow me for a moment, Chorus like, to work upon your thoughts and provoke you to the edge of repentance with a few promptings for your consideration:

1. We could begin by repenting to the Lord for our lukewarm and unrepentant spirits. Sometimes obedience begins with nothing more than a willingness to be willing to obey. Let's begin by asking God's forgiveness for the pride of our own hearts which prevents us from even being willing to obey.

2. We could move on to asking God to forgive us for seeking to take spiritual ground from the enemy, when the enemy holds that same ground in us. Ted Haggard was a leader in the fight in Colorado to ban Gay marriage. But you cannot lead a fight against sexual impurity when there is sexual impurity in your own life. You cannot cast down a spiritual stronghold while at the same time walking in it. As a Church, we could begin by repenting before the Lord for walking in the very sins and spiritual strongholds which we condemn in others.

Preparing For A Spiritual Outpouring

3. We could take another step toward genuine humility and repentance by repenting for seeking political solutions to spiritual problems, rather than seeking spiritual solutions to political (and social) problems. During the Welsh Revival of 1904 British politician (and later Prime Minister) David Lloyd-George noted that six months of the revival had done more to combat drunkenness and alcoholism (a rampant problem among the Welsh coal miners) than the "Temperance" political movement had accomplished in years of effort. When will we understand and embrace the teaching of Scripture and the lessons of revival which combine to demonstrate that God can accomplish more in two years of genuine spiritual awakening and revival than we could accomplish on our own in 20 years of conservative political action.

4. We could repent for having not reached out to "the least of these" (Matthew 25:31ff), but instead having sought the favor of the politically and financially powerful.

5. We could repent of the religious, controlling spirit of competition and "kingdom building" which seems to characterize so much of what we do in Church and ministry today.

6. Finally, we could make our repentance truly "biblical" by repenting of those same sins which Jesus rebuked among the Churches of Asia, and which the Lord, through John, recorded for our warning and instruction. We could repent of working hard but loving little as in Ephesus. We could repent of tolerating the stumbling block of compromise, as in the Church at Pergamum. We could repent of tolerating spirits of false authority and witchcraft among leaders as in the Church of Thyatira. We could repent of having fallen asleep and living off our spiritual reputation of by-gone days like the Church of Sardis, and we could repent of complacency, lukewarmness and lack of zeal as in the Church of Laodicea. But that would mean we actually wanted to do something about these sins, and that would be "expensive worship."

Chapter 8 - And Then They Repented?

"And Then They Repented"?

O.K., it's time to wrap things up. There is more that I could share, but there is a limit to what people can bear. In summary, I believe we have, indeed, entered a season of "hard" repentance for the Church both in Spokane and in our nation. God is now using His divine megaphone of pain to get the attention of a deaf church, increasing its sense of "desperation" and calling it to repentance. The pathway to revival leads through the valley of humility, brokenness, confession and repentance. Are we willing to walk through it? Or are we still looking for ways around it? Let me leave you with a starting place for your personal devotions. The following prayer of confession was penned by John Wesley some 250 years ago and has lost none of its significance over the years. Start here, make it your own, and then ask the Holy Spirit to take you deeper into the valley of repentance. Don't be afraid. The weeping of genuine repentance may last for the night, but a shout of joy comes in the morning.

"Let him who has an ear hear what the Spirit is saying to the Churches."

He is coming. Are we ready? Is your House Church a channel through which He can flow?

 Let the River flow!

Preparing For A Spiritual Outpouring

John Welsey's Prayer of Confession

Forgive them all, O Lord:
our sins of omission and our sins of commission;
The sins of our youth and the sins of our riper years;
The sins of our souls and the sins of our bodies;
Our secret and our more open sins;
Our sins of ignorance and surprise,
and our more deliberate and presumptuous sin;
The sins we have done to please ourselves,
and the sins we have done to please others;
The sins we know and remember,
and the sins we have forgotten;
The sins we have striven to hide from others,
And the sins by which we have made others offend.
Forgive them, O Lord, forgive them all for His sake,
Who died for our sins and rose for our justification,
And now stands at thy right hand to make intercession for us,
Jesus Christ our Lord.

"O Lord, Make Me Like Job"
Reflections on House Church,
Intimacy & Repentance
First Published January 9, 2007

9

I never really thought I would hear myself saying this, but here goes: I really do want to be like Job. And therein lies a story of house church, repentance and intimacy with God.

I would dare say that most Christians go through their lives hoping to avoid either reading or understanding the book of Job, much less experiencing it. And I would go on to venture that there's scarcely a believer among us whose goal or prayer is: "Lord, make me like Job." But I think that should change. And now I need to explain why (Duh!).

O.K., a quick overview. The Book of Job is a "morality play" in six parts: A "prologue," four "acts" and an "epilogue" (scholars have debated this structure for years, but this is the basic breakdown, depending on your favorite commentary). Job is a human actor in a divine drama of which he is unaware. The notion of believers as actors in a cosmic drama is alluded to by Paul in 1 Corinthians 4 where Paul refers to apostles (and by implication, other 5-Fold leadership) as "spectacles to the world". The Greek word there is *theatron* from which we get our English word "theater." (The word occurs in Acts 19:29 & 31 in an incident involving Paul, which was probably in his mind as he penned this verse). Get the idea? In the prologue (chapters 1-2) we learn how the "stage" has been set with the major players. It is there that we are specifically told, twice (Job 1:22 & 2:10), that Job was a righteous man who had not sinned. If you miss this point, the next 34 chapters can get very confusing as Job's religious paradigm regarding sin, righteousness, suffering and God's dealings with people gets seriously challenged. Job is getting divinely set up for a radical paradigm shift.

Job's Counselors

Job gets some "help" with his paradigm shift from three

Preparing For A Spiritual Outpouring

"friends" and a stranger. These four people combine to communicate one message: *"You've sinned, and that's why God has allowed/done this"* (O.K., If you're a Calvinist, God did it; if you're an Arminian, He simply allowed it). God doesn't do this to people who haven't sinned" (remember the important point I made above). Through four long and sometimes tedious "acts" these four "counselors" repeat their arguments and thereby reveal their "religious boxes" into which Job simply doesn't fit.

Bildad the Shuhite (known as the shortest man in the Bible - after all, he was only "shu-hite" - O.K., you may now groan appropriately) is the "traditionalist," always appealing to what the fathers have said about the situation because there was nothing new to be learned. He is a traditionalist and he looks back in history to find what others have already said. He has a high regard for truth and sees it as inherited, not to be messed with, something wrestled over by the elders, handed down to those eager for wisdom, and eventually passed on to the next generation. (I want to thank Andrew Jones, otherwise known as "TallSkinnyKiwi" for his excellent article "The Skinny on Post Modernity - Part 1" for some insights into Job. His quotes are in italic in this section).

Zophar is the "rationalist" who appeals to rational wisdom and hints that Job is "witless" or stupid. He also gives a formula that "if" Job does certain things, then a favorable outcome will result. I would add that this also makes Zophar an unwitting model for what I call "Christian magicians," believers who are looking for "magic formulas" which they can use to manipulate God: "If you do A, B and C, God will always do D". Such people are the "Harry Potters" of the church who regard the things of God as formulas to be followed or spells to be cast in order to get the desired result.

Eliphaz is the "mystic" in the bunch whose "authority" is to appeal to his experiences to prove his point. He had a dream and his hair stood on end. A spirit appeared. This was proof enough. He sees God as One Who "performs wonders that

Chapter 9 - O Lord, Make Me Like Job

cannot be fathomed".

Then there's **Elihu**, the "stranger" who turns out to be the "theologian" of the group. You know the type. The young Turk fresh out of seminary whose passion exceeds his wisdom and whose response is something like, *"How dare you question God. Don't you know this was all dealt with in Book I, Chapter I of the Lewis Battles Ford edition of Calvin's Institutes, not to mention Berkhof's Systematic Theology?"* (Don't worry. He'll grow up!).

These four "counselors" combined together to present Job with "explanations which didn't explain" and which left Job with a "pain in the mind" (to use Leslie Newbigin's two expressions) which would not go away. The answers given by his "friends" were the standard "religious" answers of the prevailing religious paradigm as they understood it. Andrew Jones observes, *"A funny thing about the Book of Job is that each guy, with such radically differing thought processes, comes to the same conclusion - Job has sinned and is therefore suffering. Even funnier is the fact that all three men are wrong. The truth in this case is something more complicated and mysterious. But watching them think is worth the exercise since they represent how people think in general."*

My perspective is that Job's counselors were all "right" according to the prevailing religious paradigm of the day, a paradigm which Job probably shared up until this fateful series of events. But none of their right answers were valid in Job's situation (hence, their frustration and Job's despair). They were offering "boxed" answers to an "outside" the box situation. Like many believers today, they were giving Job the "right answers" to the wrong question. They wanted intimacy with God, but only on terms of their own understanding, which was now being seriously challenged.

Job was on a spiritual journey that no one seemed to understand or appreciate, including Job, his wife, his friends and a significant number of readers and commentators in the

Preparing For A Spiritual Outpouring

3500 years since then! And in the face of the unknown our first and most consistent tendency is to fall back into "truisms" - answers that are "usually true" and have served us in the past. But not now. It isn't until God makes a personal appearance, thirty eight chapters into this play, and reveals Himself both to Job and (we may assume) his inquisitors, that we begin to understand the truth of what is taking place. God then spends four chapters revealing His greatness and exposing Job's (and our) insignificance: *"I'm God. You're not. Get used to it."* How profound is this message? Well, after 3500 years, we still haven't "gotten used to it". Hmmmmm.

O.K., I know I'm passing quickly and lightly over a lot of material (like 42 chapters worth). I'm moving quickly because I want to get to "the punch line" which is found in the "epilogue" in Chapter 42.

The Epilogue (And Punch Line)

Then Job answered the Lord, and said, *"I know that Thou canst do all things, And that no purpose of Thine can be thwarted. 'Who is this that hides counsel without knowledge?' Therefore I have declared that which I did not understand, things too wonderful for me, which I did not know. 'Hear, now, and I will speak; I will ask Thee, and do Thou instruct me.' I have heard of Thee by the hearing of the ear; But now my eye sees Thee; therefore I retract, and I repent in dust and ashes."*

The five "poetical" books of the Old Testament are all about "intimacy" with God, but on His terms, not ours. The Book of Job teaches us the sovereignty of God, sovereignty over His created order and over human suffering. An understanding of the sovereignty and greatness of God should lead us to the worship and fear of Him, hence the book Psalms which follows. Worship and fear give way to wisdom (Proverbs), give us understanding and stability to confront, understand and overcome the seeming "vanity" of life (Ecclesiastes) while challenging and encouraging us to pursue and respond to God as one pursues and responds to a lover of our soul (Song of

Chapter 9 - O Lord, Make Me Like Job

Songs).

In the epilogue, Job comes to his personal realization of the greatness and sovereignty of God. It is a rude but necessary awakening. We see this realization unfold as Job quotes God's own words back to Him, *'Who is this that hides counsel without knowledge?' Job comes to the realization that he has "declared that which I did not understand"*. The sense of the Hebrew here is that Job had "boldly proclaimed, held forth and published" things about God regarding which he really knew nothing at all. What a humbling realization that must have been for Job can be seen in the words which follow next. Job quotes God's own words again, "'Hear, now, and I will speak; I will ask Thee, and do Thou instruct me.'" Earlier, God had "invited" Job to teach Him. Now, at last, Job understands who is the teacher and who is the student. That's a humbling realization for the "know-it-alls" among us (ahem!).

So, where's the "punch line" (As my daughter would say, *"Wait for it dad, wait for it!"*)? In verses 5-6: *"I have heard of Thee by the hearing of the ear; But now my eye sees Thee; therefore I retract, and I repent in dust and ashes"*. Three things happen here that we need to notice.

The first is that Job comes to a new understanding of who God is. He moves from a knowledge of God that was handed down by what he had heard from others ("by the hearing of the ear") to a knowledge of God that was personal, experiential and, yes, even intimate (ha! told you to wait for it!).

The second thing that happened is that Job had one of those rare moments of personal introspection when he realized how wrong he had been about God and the result was genuine grief and personal self-loathing. The NASB rendering of "retract" represents (I suspect) more modern psychology than Hebrew nuance. The older KJV is closer to the sense of the Hebrew: *"I abhor myself"*. If you have never had one of those moments alone with God when you weep the tears of the broken hearted over a personal realization of how wrong you have been about

Preparing For A Spiritual Outpouring

God - and how you have shared that ignorance with others in a very authoritative manner - then let me be the first to tell you that your journey into genuine intimacy has a "road not taken" that is just waiting for you.

The third thing that happened to Job is the result of the other two: He had a genuine change of heart, mind and attitude toward God. In other words, he repented. There are two primary Hebrew words for "repent" in the Old Testament. The first and most common is "*shuwb*" which simply means "to turn," resulting in a change of behavior or direction. The second word is "*nacham*" which means "to have a change of heart, attitude, mind or purpose." This second word is the one used here in Job 42:6. Based upon what he had experienced and learned about God, Job had a change of heart & mind about God and His dealings in his own life, resulting (I believe) in greater personal intimacy with God.

O.K., let me try to summarize what all of this has to do with our personal journey into greater intimacy with God. From Job's experience I come away with the lesson that personal repentance and growth in our intimacy with God are related, even inseparable. Without a spirit of humility and repentance there can be no genuine intimacy with God, because such intimacy is a function of and somehow dependent upon our willingness and ability to humble ourselves, repent and learn "new" things about the God Whom we worship. These "new" things we learn may be as old as Job (or as C.H Spurgeon said, "If it's new it's probably heresy"), but they are new to us and our experience. And embracing them may require profound personal humility - maybe even a moment of personal self-loathing - and genuine personal repentance.

O, Lord, Make Me Like Job (?)

O.K., now we're back where we started, but hopefully having gained some insight during the journey. Let's be real. None of us (except those manic depressives and sado-masochists who really do need a hug, followed by counseling and Prozac!) want

Chapter 9 - O Lord, Make Me Like Job

to experience what Job experienced. But I am convinced that a loving, sovereign and omnipotent God understood that such was the path required in order for Job to achieve the degree of spiritual insight, humility and, eventually, intimacy that God wanted for Job. With all due respect, that was his "best life now" (see my article *"Umbrellas, Crosses & The Kingdom of God,"* posted in our e-letter archives on our website).

What I want from Job, and what I would hope we would all want, is the humility and willingness to repent of my wrong understandings of God and embrace the "new" ones He wants to offer me. My goal is intimacy with God, and the path to that intimacy leads through self-awareness, humility and repentance. I only hope (and pray!) that it won't take Job's experiences to get me to my destination.

Job had his religious paradigm radically shaken. How about you? If you are part of the house church/organic church movement I suspect that your paradigm has already been (or is being) radically shaken. I suspect you've already encountered some things which you have had to repent over. If not, you might want to prepare yourself for "the road not taken" (and you might also want to check out Wolfgang Simson's *"5 Steps of Apostolic Migration"* posted on our website under "House Church Resources").

The road into genuine intimacy with God will look different for each person, because God deals with each of us as individuals. There are no formulas or programs for this. Intimacy is personal and relational, not formulaic or programmatic. But occasionally you can recognize people who are on this journey. My two sure-fire indicators that I have encountered a fellow traveler on this journey are these. **First,** when they think no one is watching you will see them walk with a limp, the left-over reminder of a divine encounter that changed their life and started them on this journey into intimacy. **Secondly,** when they think no one is listening you will occasionally hear them whisper a quiet prayer: *"Father, forgive me. I had heard of Thee by the hearing of the ear; But now my eye sees Thee; therefore*

Preparing For A Spiritual Outpouring

I abhor myself, and I repent in dust and ashes."

Welcome to this amazing journey into house church, humility, intimacy and preparation for a season of spiritual outpouring with God. And so long as we're together . . . feel free to limp.

He is coming. Are we ready? Is your House Church a channel through which He can flow?

 Let the River flow!

"He Who Has An Ear, Let Him Hear What The Spirit Says To The Churches"

10

First Published May 2, 2007

What I am about to relate will be a paradigm bender for many of you, and your tendency will be to dismiss it as foolishness. As a "recovering rationalist" I understand. Others of you will respond with what I can only describe as a "fatal familiarity," characterized by an attitude of "Oh, yeah, been there, done that. No big deal". For these, their "familiarity" with the supernatural will prove "fatal" due to their failure to appreciate the gravity of what occurred. There is a large kernel of wisdom behind the ol' adage that "familiarity breeds contempt." In order to appreciate the significance of what I am about to relate, you will need to avoid both extremes.

The Meeting

The following took place at a recent house church gathering, but I will not divulge where, when or who. I will only say that I know and trust the people involved, people not given to "pushing the envelope" or "flights of fancy". The meeting lasted approximately four hours. What I am about to relate began roughly an hour into the gathering. According to half of the people who were present and actually witnessed this, three angels appeared, each bearing a specific message.

The First Angel. According to those present who witnessed this, the first angel was clothed in crimson and purple and had a regal nature about him. His message, as recorded by one person present, was as follows:

"This is what the spirit has to say to the 1st Church: Listen! The 1st angel of the church first established in the Lord says this. Repent, for my heart is broken, for I have broken the staff of correction over the backs of my sheep who long for different pastures and whose heart is fat on that which is not holy, for I will now let them pursue their own lusts and (I will now) stand out of the way!"

71

Preparing For A Spiritual Outpouring

The Second Angel. According to those who witnessed this, the second angel was clothed humbly and "non-descriptly" with simple robes. His message was as follows:

"The 2nd angel has to say in a still small voice, be quiet, for only those who seek to drink from the still small brook and who are not afraid of persecution, who love the Lord more than life and thirst not for the glory and the big things that profit only the flesh, who hunger for intimacy, shall enter in! For in such is true power found - in the quiet clearings where the River of God's brook quietly murmurs shall peace and purpose be found. Clothe yourselves in humility, for I shall be found there in peace and tranquility!"

The Third Angel. The third angel was . . . well . . . read on:

"When the 3rd angel approached me I trembled in fear (!) for he is an all consuming fire. His eyes are ablaze with God's glory and his robes are a burning furnace - for he is fresh from the Lord's Presence, shrouded with His glory and holiness! And his presence is a terrible thing, for he has to say: 'Go tell my people to Repent, for they have lost their fear of the Lord, they no longer desire to hear what He truly has to say (It will cost you everything!). Holiness - Holiness - Holiness. Be Holy, for I am holy! Tremble in fear for I am coming!'"

The Meaning

The people involved in this meeting/visitation were deeply affected both then and for several days afterwards (well, duh!). One of them called me on the verge of tears, *"I've been pondering this all day. Maurice, what does this mean?"* Good question. I believe it means several things, and I want to try and summarize what I think is happening.

First, throughout Scripture angelic appearances for the purpose of delivering messages are significant events. It is like placing an exclamation point at the end of a divine sentence; like driving a "stake of remembrance" in the ground so we will

Chapter 10 - He Who Has An Ear, Let Him Hear

not forget or take lightly what He has said. A good example of this is found in Daniel Chapter 9 where Daniel prays for wisdom, knowledge and discernment. God answers by sending an angel to deliver a message to Daniel. I have written about this episode in my fasting devotional book, *"Not By Bread Alone"* (page 148). Here is what I wrote there about this event: *"God delights to make Himself known to those who seek Him. But Daniel's experience also teaches us about the gravity of the things which God reveals, and this reflects God's Holiness. Although God delights to reveal Himself to those who seek Him, He requires that those who receive His revelation exercise humility in prayer, that they respond to His revelation with prudent and circumspect behavior and with discernment ("What does this mean, and how does God want me to use this?"). We are to treat God's revelations as holy, because they partake of His character."* As in the case of Daniel, angelic visitations are intended to emphasize the "gravitas" of both the moment and the message.

Second, God is still calling His people to repentance (two of the three angelic messages contained exhortations to repent). As one of the participants told me later, *"The Lord seemed to be emphasizing the message of repentance which He has given you recently."* God has been calling His people to repent, but they have resisted the "staff of correction" and so He is preparing to send them one of the worst forms of judgment; He is going to stand aside and let them have their own way: *"I will now let them pursue their own lusts and (I will now) stand out of the way!"* It is a terrible day when God gives us over to the lusts and desires of our own heart.

This encounter reminds me of the angelic messages to the seven churches of Asia. And along that line, the "1st angel" of the "1st church" could suggest the Church of Ephesus (first of the seven churches of Asia). What was the problem in the Church of Ephesus? It was a church which had substituted activity for intimacy and had left their first love. Hmmmm. This seems to lead to the next point (a convenient segue).

Preparing For A Spiritual Outpouring

Third, God is calling His people to quietude and listening to His still small voice. This speaks of pursuing humility and intimacy. Are we listening, or are we too busy pursuing "great things" to hear the still small voice?

Fourth, God is calling His Church to holiness, and He is going to do this by returning "the fear of the Lord" to the Church. It is a terrible but needed "gift". How serious is this? Read the last line again: "Tremble in fear for I am coming!"

Tilt!

O.K.. at this point your spiritual pinball machine should be on "TILT" (feel free to sing "Pinball Wizard" from the rock musical "Tommy" by the Who at this point. It'll buy you a little time while you work to spiritually assimilate all of this!). This is a lot to absorb, but I think I understand where we are. We are entering a season of divine visitation and God is driving a stake in the ground (one of those "Remember this day!" moments). He is calling His Church back to repentance, to intimacy and to holiness. These three messages are not new. We've heard them before over the past several months. But apparently we need a "refresher course" on how important they are to the heart of God in this unfolding season, so He chose to repeat them via a "delivery vehicle" designed to burn them indelibly into our spiritual consciousness. Three prophetic exhortations delivered with three divine exclamation points for emphasis. Get it? Got it? Believe it?!

A season of divine visitation is unfolding, a season built upon repentance, intimacy and holiness. Where it goes from here only He and He alone knows. He's God. We're not. Get over it! The River of God's Spirit, the River of Ezekiel 47, is preparing to flow in power . . . and holiness, the likes of which we have never seen before, at least not in the living memory of the Church. Are you and your house church a vessel through which He can flow? Are you pursuing repentance, intimacy and holiness? If not, now would be a good time to start.

Chapter 10 - He Who Has An Ear, Let Him Hear

Get ready, and *"Tremble in fear for I am coming!"*

"He who has an ear, let him hear what the Spirit says to the churches."

He is coming. Are we ready? Is your House Church a channel through which He can flow?

 Let the River flow!

Preparing For A Spiritual Outpouring

Defragging House Church
Part 1: The DNA of the Coming Move of God
First Published May 9, 2007

11

I recently acquired a copy of Alan Hirsch's newest book, *"The Forgotten Ways"*. All I can say is "wow". The book is a must read and I hope to write a thorough review of it in an upcoming newsletter. Leonard Sweet (*"Post Modern Pilgrims"* and *"The Gospel According To Starbucks"*) wrote the forward to the book and entitled it Have you Defragged Recently. *"Sometimes our hard drives need defragmenting", he writes. "Data entered on our hard drive isn't always done neatly. The more files you have, and the more programs you download, the more your hard drive gets scrambled by confusing, scattered, random inputs that get sprayed over lots of space. Computer crashes, power outages, and stalled programs just add to the fragmentation . . . . Christianity has undergone untold crashes and clashes in the past two thousand years. In the last five hundred years its original hard drive has wiped out so many times, especially in the west, that it has almost ground to a halt."*

Welcome to house church (or simple church, or organic church, or emerging church, or whatever moniker you want to assign to this recently constituted band of sojourners). To use Leonard Sweet's analogy, if House Church were a computer hard drive, its usefulness would be somewhat minimal except for games of "spiritual spider solitaire". We have become clogged and fragmented with failed & junk programs, many of which need to be "uninstalled" and the rest need to be "defragged". Most of the current participants in the house church movement have come out of traditional churches, and they have brought their jumbled, clogged hard drives with them, seeking some new mother board to plug into, thinking that a new board will solve their problems. It doesn't occur to them that it's the internal hard drive they're carrying around with them that's the real problem. It needs to be cleaned & defragged; assuming of course that it is even salvageable and not in need of junking in favor of a brand new one.

Preparing For A Spiritual Outpouring

I wish I knew how to do it. Defragging the house church movement, that is. I confess I really don't. But why let a little thing like ignorance and incompetence stop us, right?! So let's pioneer on and see if we can make sense of this whole thing. Over the next several weeks I plan (hope might be a better word) to offer a series of articles under the banner of "Defragging House Church". In this series we will examine several issues facing house church. This week I want to examine "The DNA of the Coming Move of God". Future articles will deal with such things as intimacy versus outreach, the return of Gnosticism (coming to a house church near you!), re-thinking leadership, signs, wonders and other distractions, and more. So, without further "a do" let's get started defragging house church.

The DNA of the Coming Move of God

O.K. We have a challenge at the outset here. In order to fully appreciate the following discussion you need to have read last week's letter. So, if you haven't already done so, why not take a moment and do that right now (you'll find it in Chapter 10, page 71).

O.K. Welcome back (you did read the letter, right?). While you're processing what you just read (hey, it took me a week!), let me ask you a question. What is it about your house church that is worth duplicating for the next five house church generations? What is it about what you are doing that you would want God to rapidly multiply into the lives of others? Is the spiritual DNA of your present expression of *ekklesia* (I really wish we could get away from the English word "church") something worth passing on ad infinitum? And what would the ekklesia of Jesus look like if that were to happen?

Let's start with a definition from our friends at Wikipedia: *"Deoxyribonucleic acid, or DNA is a nucleic acid molecule that contains the genetic instructions used in the development and functioning of all living organisms. The main role of DNA is the long-term storage of information and it is often compared to a*

Chapter 11 - Defragging House Church

set of blueprints, since DNA contains the instructions needed to construct other components of cells, such as proteins and RNA molecules." Whew! O.K., here's the point. The *ekklesia* of Jesus, including your house church expression of it, is a living organism. It, too, has a "spiritual DNA," a "spiritual blueprint" for reproduction and growth that will determine what the end product of that reproduction looks like - just as your own biological DNA determined how tall you would be and whether your hair would be black or your eyes blue. Good DNA produces good outcomes. Bad DNA produces bad outcomes. The lesson is simple: What is the spiritual DNA of your house church and what is it producing that is worth multiplying?

Now, back to last week's letter (which I hope you've worked through by now). The "big lesson" which I took away from that experience was this: We are entering a profound season of divine visitation and spiritual outpouring during which the River of Ezekiel 47, the River of God's Spirit, is going to flow with great power and blessing. And at the outset God is seeking to sow a basic spiritual DNA into this unfolding move of God's Spirit which will manifest in and flow through house churches. This DNA consists of three genetic characteristics. Here they are: 1) Repentance, 2) Intimacy and 3) Holiness (& the fear of the Lord). How important are these for this coming move? Important enough for God to communicate them via "special delivery," thereby guaranteeing an indelible impression on those who heard and received. So, let me touch on each of these in its turn.

DNA Trait # 1: Repentance

"If the foundations are destroyed,
what shall the righteous do"
Psalm 11:3

The ancient Hebrew Psalmist (David) understood something which we have forgotten, namely, that certain things are "foundational". A truth is "foundational" if its removal jeopardizes whatever you are seeking to build. In the Church of

Preparing For A Spiritual Outpouring

God, repentance is a "foundational" truth. Remove it, and the very nature and existence of the Church is threatened. Exactly how foundational is repentance to the biblical message? That's easy. It IS the biblical message. Don't take my word for it. Listen to the words of Jesus (and John the Baptist): *"Repent, for the kingdom of heaven is at hand."* (Matthew 3:2; 4:17; Mark 1:14-15). The "unsettling" thing about Jesus' message of repentance is that He directed it at the religious believers of His day, the very people whom the Old Testament Scriptures named as God's chosen people. If God's chosen people in Jesus' day were in need of repentance, what (other than our pride) makes us think that His people today are somehow exempt from that same message? Unfortunately, repentance has become the "lost heart" of God's people today. One seldom hears messages on the need for personal or corporate repentance from sin. And yet when we look at the New Testament there are some 58 references to the need to repent. "Repent" is the most frequent instruction given by the risen Christ to the 7 Churches of Asia in Revelation chapters 2 & 3 (occurring 6 times). Repentance is a matter close to God's heart.

What Is Repentance?

What exactly is "repentance"? The concept of repentance in the life of God's Old Testament people was most often expressed by the use of two Hebrew words. The first Hebrew word for repentance, _Nacham_, describes a "grieving" which produces a change of attitude, heart or disposition, a change of mind, a change of purpose, or a change of one's conduct. The second Hebrew word for repentance is Shuwb the basic meaning of which is "movement back to the point of departure". _Shuwb_ is the twelfth most frequently used Hebrew verb in the OT. It occurs 1,060 times, with an additional eight times in biblical Aramaic (where it is spelled tuwb). The word is used for simple physical motion about 270 times. _Shuwb_ occurs most often in the book of Jeremiah (111 times) where it serves as Jeremiah's favorite word for repentance. _Shuwb_ literally means "to turn and go in a different direction." A good example of these two words

Chapter 11 - Defragging House Church

being used together in a way which highlights their unique meanings is found in Exodus 13:17, "Now it came about when Pharaoh had let the people go, that God did not lead them by the way of the land of the Philistines, even though it was near; for God said, 'Lest the people change their minds when they see war, and they return to Egypt.'"

The plight of Israel coming out of Egypt gives us a practical example of "repentance," namely, people having a "change of heart" (*nacham*) followed by "turning in a different direction" (*shuwb*). The context is the Exodus from Egypt. The Hebrew people had been slaves in Egypt for some 400 years. Now they were leaving Egypt on their way to the Promised Land. But they were unprepared for the prospect of battle or war. So, God led them in such a way (basically He took them "the long way around") in order to avoid war. Why? Because God knew that the difficulties of a battle might cause the people to grieve and have a "change of heart" about the whole deal, causing them to abandon their purpose and literally "turn around" and go back to Egypt. This incident gives us a basic practical example and explanation of "repentance": Repentance is a profound change of thinking or attitude that results in a profound change of direction.

Many Christians make the mistake of thinking that "repentance" is all about repenting of sin. While this is an important reason and occasion for repentance, it is not the only reason and occasion for repentance. For example, repentance is one of the dominant themes of the book of Jeremiah, God calling His people to repent of their sin and rebellion and return to Him. But in Chapter 15 God tells Jeremiah, *"Therefore, thus says the LORD, 'If you return, then I will restore you-- Before Me you will stand; And if you extract the precious from the worthless, You will become My spokesman. They for their part may turn to you, But as for you, you must not turn to them.'"* (Jeremiah 15:19) The word "return" in this verse is Jeremiah's word for "repent". God is telling Jeremiah that if he will repent - turn his focus away from what is happening around him and turn towards the Lord as his sole focus - then God will restore Jeremiah (literally,

Preparing For A Spiritual Outpouring

"I will turn to you") and cause Jeremiah to stand before Him. In essence, God is telling Jeremiah that repentance on his part will result in greater intimacy with God. Think of it as Jeremiah turning to God and God responding by turning to Jeremiah, with the result that both get more "face time" together.

In this unfolding season of spiritual outpouring (of which the house church movement will be an integral part) God is seeking a repentant people. He wants a people whose first impulse is to repent by turning their focus away from anything and everything that distracts from intimacy and holiness with God and to focus their attention solely upon Him. What does this mean for your house church? Simple. Are the people in your house church still focused upon murmuring about the failings of the traditional or institutional church? Then it's time to repent, and to get your focus upon the God Whose church it is in spite of its many failings. It's time to focus upon what God has called you to be and do, not upon what He has called you to leave. Are people in your house church still carrying around the wounds of past church experiences? Then it is time to repent, and to stop focusing upon your woundedness and to begin focusing upon the LORD our healer Who heals the broken hearted (Psalm 147:3). Are you starting to get the picture here? Repentance is not just about repenting from sin, it is also about getting our focus off of those things which distract us from the Lord and intimacy with Him. It is about restoring the Lord and "the beauty of His holiness" as our focus. Is a spirit of repentance part of the DNA of your house church? If not, now would be a good time to start.

DNA Trait # 2: Intimacy

> "When Thou didst say, 'Seek My face,'
> my heart said to Thee,
> 'Thy face, O Lord, I shall seek'"
> Psalm 27:8

Let me shake and bend your paradigm a little with this statement: You cannot have genuine intimacy with God without genuine repentance from those things which distract your focus from Him. *Genuine repentance is the doorway to greater intimacy with God.* We see this reflected in Psalm 24 when the Psalmist says, *"Who may ascend into the hill of the LORD? And who may stand in His holy place? He who has clean hands and a pure heart, Who has not lifted up his soul to falsehood, And has not sworn deceitfully."* (Psalm 24:3-4) To stand in God's "holy place" is to have intimate fellowship with him, but to get there one must have "clean hands and a pure heart". How do we get clean hands and a pure heart? Through repentance, the confession of sin and the turning away from those things which fill our hearts and hands and turn our focus away from Him. When the Church at Ephesus in Revelation 2:4 left their first love and lost their intimacy with Jesus, the answer to restoring that love and that intimacy wasn't better worship music or even a better sermon. Rather, it was repentance. When the tepid believers of Laodicea discovered Jesus on the outside of their church seeking entrance (wow, talk about lost intimacy!), the answer to restored intimacy was simple: ". . . be zealous, therefore, and repent." (Revelation 3:19-20) Much of what passes for "intimacy" in the church today is "cheap intimacy" - "intimacy" without repentance. "Cheap intimacy" is like "cheap worship," an emotionally stimulating experience which costs us little or nothing. No self-examination, no death to self, no repentance from sin or distractions, no discernment. Just more words, more music . . . and more distractions.

Is genuine intimacy with God part of the DNA of your house church? In addition to repentance, genuine intimacy requires significant amounts of "face time" between us and God. Are you as a house church pursuing genuine intimacy with God. Are you spending a significant amount of "face time" with God as a group - praying, worshiping, waiting in silence, and, yes, repenting before the Lord?

DNA Trait # 3: Holiness & The Fear of God

"Therefore, having these promises, beloved, let us cleanse ourselves from all defilement of flesh and spirit, perfecting

Preparing For A Spiritual Outpouring

holiness in the fear of God." (2 Corinthians 7:1)

Do you see the pattern building here? Allow me to 'splain it. Genuine repentance (DNA Trait #1) leads to genuine intimacy with God. And Genuine intimacy (DNA Trait #2) with God leads to greater holiness (DNA Trait #3) before God. Funny how that works. You'd think God has a plan here!

O.K., we need to take a moment and define "holiness." Here goes: *"Holiness is that perfection and attribute of God's nature whereby He is separated from sin and evil, and is singularly devoted to seeking His own glory."* Stephen Charnock, the 17th century English Puritan divine, summed up God's holiness best when he observed, *"Power is God's hand or arm, omniscience His eye, mercy His bowels, eternity His duration, but holiness is His beauty."* For the believer who shares the divine nature (2 Peter 1:4) and is commanded to ". . . be holy, for I am holy" (1 Peter 1:16), holiness exists in two parts. On the one hand, holiness has to do with our separation and purity from evil and moral sin. On the other hand, holiness has to do with our being devoted to serving and pursuing God's glory in genuine moral purity. Legalism is not holiness. Rules such as "I don't drink, dance, smoke or chew, or run around with girls who do" is not holiness. It is the rules of legalism masquerading as holiness. Genuine holiness is us manifesting the very nature of the God Who is holy and Who invites us to the same through repentance and greater intimacy with Himself. And no set of rules can ever produce that.

What interests me in this season is how the third angelic message (see last week's e-letter) corresponds to the above verse in 2 Corinthians. In the coming spiritual outpouring, God intends to mark His church with the DNA of holiness by returning "the fear of the Lord" to His people. How is He going to do this? I don't know. What I do know is that the history of spiritual outpourings makes it clear that God is able. If you want a reminder, go back and read Chapter 6, page 43, *"House Church Reflections: When The Holy Spirit Comes . . . Via Inter Library Loan"*.

Chapter 11 - Defragging House Church

Summary - "You Can't Teach Your Way To Better DNA"

I hope this doesn't come to you as a shock, but most Churches in America are led by teachers, not pastors. Being the good rationalists that we are, we genuinely believe that the key to right thinking and behavior is good teaching. So, the battle cry of the "pastor search committee" of the average church is something like this, "We need someone who is an excellent Bible teacher." And that is, indeed, what they usually get. A teacher. Now, don't get me wrong. Teaching is a valuable and worthy gift in the Church. But the "blind spot" of a teacher is the belief that all problems in the life of the individual and the church can be solved with better teaching. A gifted teacher has never met a problem that he (or she) couldn't teach his way out of. Are people in your church having marital problems? Bring in the teachers to teach "biblical marriage." Is giving down and stewardship a problem? Bring in the financial management teachers to teach biblical financial principles. But marriages continue to fail at an alarming and growing rate, and Christian giving as a percentage of income continues to fall (35% in 35 years). Why? Because as valuable as good teaching is, you cannot teach your way to better DNA! Good Bible teaching is the "ordinary" work of the Church, a task given to and performed by gifted 5-Fold teachers as part of the "normal" life of the Church. But changing the DNA of the Church represents the extra-ordinary work of the Holy Spirit.

O.K., you say, *"If you can't teach your way to better DNA, why are you teaching us about this?!"* (Hmmm. Good question, grasshopper. And when you can take the pebble from my hand, it will be time for you to go. Oooops, sorry, old Kung Fu rerun just kicked in). I am "teaching" you this so you will understand what God is about to do in and through His church. And if this is what God is about to do, you and I have an opportunity to actively pursue it and to willingly participate. The rest is up to Him. God is about to visit His Church and indelibly imprint new (but old) DNA upon her character. Why? So that in the House Church generations yet to be born we will multiply and reproduce believers and churches where repentance, intimacy and holiness are "the norm," just as Zechariah foresaw: *"In that day there will be inscribed on the bells of the horses, 'HOLY TO THE LORD.' And the cooking pots in the Lord's house will be like the bowls before the altar. And every cooking pot in Jerusalem and in Judah will be holy to the Lord of hosts; and all who sacrifice will come and take of them. And there will no longer be a Canaanite in the house of the Lord of hosts in that day."* (Zechariah 14:20-21)

A season of divine visitation is unfolding, a season built upon repentance, intimacy and holiness. Where it goes from here only He and He alone knows. He's God. We're not. Get over it! The River of God's Spirit, the River of Ezekiel 47, is preparing to flow in power . . . and holiness, the likes of which we have never seen before, at least not in the living memory of the Church. Are you and your house church a vessel through which He can flow? Are you pursuing repentance, intimacy and holiness? If not, now would be a good time to start.

He is coming. Are we ready? Is your House Church a channel through which He can flow?

 Let the River flow!

House Church Reflections From A Beach On Maui

12

First Published August 22, 2007

Yep. We're Back!

For those of you who have been "out of the loop", my wife & I spent just over a week in Maui. The trip was the gift of a house church friend whose family lives there and does property development on the island. For a week we had a lovely condo in Kihei to ourselves along with a car (a Mustang convertible, if you must know). It took us three days just to "unwind" and realize we were really there and had nothing we "need to do". We found a nice stretch of beach to sit on, attended a luau (I was disappointed that there was no "boar's tooth ceremony" like in South Pacific, but hey, it was good), ate too much and did nothing for 7 whole days! Yep, its been a while and we were in serious need of this. Mahalo, Doug.

Two Books

One should always be careful what one takes to read while on vacation. My wife took a copy of *"The Heavenly Man,"* the story of Brother Yun of the Chinese house church movement. I took my copy of *"The Shaping of Things To Come"* by Frost and Hirsch. It can be a dangerous combination, two convicting books and too much time on your hands to read and think about them. And that's where I found myself. Somewhere between a Mai Tai and a Piña Colada (O.K., no cheap shot jokes. I'm confessing here, so cut me some slack), I had a realization which cut me to the quick. *"The Heavenly Man"* is an inside account of the Chinese house church movement as seen through the life experience of one man who was (is) one of its distinctive leaders. From this book I came away with the deep realization that the Chinese house church movement is essentially a missionary movement made up of martyrs who have counted the cost and chosen to pay it. Frost and Hirsch make the point that the western church is an institution that needs to become a missionary movement. And there's the contrast between west and east. It is the contrast between a

Preparing For A Spiritual Outpouring

missionary movement of martyrs and an institution of consumers in search of a mission. Just to add guilt to our sense of conviction, the Chinese house church movement has made a commitment to take the gospel "Back to Jerusalem". And what lies between China and Jerusalem? Ninety percent (90%) of the Muslim world. That's right. The Chinese church has chosen the path of missions and martyrdom, and they know it. The western church, on the other hand, has chosen to take the gospel "Back to Starbucks". What lies between us and Starbucks? Every WalMart in town. The "good news" is that if our Starbucks strategy fails, we can always open a Café in the Church lobby and declare "mission accomplished" (O.K., in the interest of honesty and "full disclosure," I am writing this while sitting at a Christian Café sipping my overpriced *"caffè e latte"*).

Brother Yun's observations regarding the western Church are poignant and heart breaking (he and his family are now German citizens - a long story you'll read in the book). One of his first experiences in the western church was to be attacked by "bible teachers from California" who attacked him and called him a fraud, a hoax and a stool pigeon for the Chinese government. I suppose that's what the church of Laodicea does when rudely and unceremoniously aroused from its slumber. We're a surly bunch when our comfort levels are challenged by authentic believers who have lived lives of little or no comfort.

As you can probably discern, the combination of Brother Yun's story and Frost & Hirsch's observations regarding the "post-Christendom" church (read the book) touched me very deeply. They forced me to ask questions about myself and about the House Church movement of which I am a part. Questions like, *"What are we doing? Why are we meeting? What's our mission? Where are we going?"* Because you and I are a house church or a simple church doesn't mean we have avoided the pitfall of being "an institution in search of a mission." The deadly spiritual calcification of institutionalism can occur among 12 people meeting in a living room just as easily as among 1,200 people meeting in an auditorium. Is it

88

Chapter 12 - House Church Reflections

occurring among you?

A Wake Up Call In Maui

While we were in Maui a couple of other things happened of note. First, one morning the Holy Spirit woke me up at around 4:45 in the morning to pray. As I sat in the early morning quiet of the condo, praying and watching the sunrise, the Lord spoke very clearly: *"I am going to give My Church an Isaiah 6 experience of my holiness."* The word was as clear as any I have ever received. The reference, of course, is to the prophet Isaiah's vision of God in the temple found in Isaiah 6:1-6. I'll have more to say on this passage in an up-coming e-letter, but for now, let me make this observation. Isaiah 6:1-6 tells us four critical things which each of us needs to know: 1) It tells us who God is, 2) it tells us who we are in relation to Him; 3) it tells us what He has done for us; 4) it tells us what we are to do in response. To summarize, it was Isaiah's dramatic encounter with the holiness/fear of God which led to his obedience.

The other item of note while we were in the islands was a personal visit to the Arizona Memorial on Oahu outside of Pearl Harbor. As an amateur history buff who has read Gordon Prange's definitive history of the events leading up to Pearl Harbor (*"At Dawn We Slept"*) several times, this was a "personal pilgrimage" for me. It felt like the closure of a chapter. There are actually three memorials there. The first is the Arizona. The second is the battleship Missouri, on whose decks the Instruments of Surrender were signed in Tokyo bay, ending the war in the Pacific. The third is the U.S.S. Bowfin, a submarine which saw action in the Pacific. Walking through the "garden" of memorial markers to submarine crews which were lost in action (often with no trace) with the inscription "Eternally On Patrol" was a thought provoking and somber experience that cannot help but cause one to reflect.

Memorials are markers created by one generation in the hope of reminding future generations of what happened and why.

Preparing For A Spiritual Outpouring

Like stones placed and left in the river Jordan by the Israelites, they are intended to cause future generations to ask: "What mean these stones?" Civilizations and people are known by their "memorial stones." But memorials are just that - memorials. The Arizona was once a battleship. But no longer. The Missouri was once a battleship. But no longer. If war should break out, neither would be of any use.

There is a lesson here that dawned on me as I spent a long morning reflecting on all that I saw. Physical warfare mirrors spiritual warfare in many ways. Physical memorials mirror a spiritual reality in many ways too. The best I can do is to sum it up like this: Our history is our heritage, but it is not our destiny. The warfare of our generation, spiritually speaking, is quite different from the warfare of our fathers and grandfathers. Let me explain what I mean. For a time after I wrote my book on the Welsh revival of 1904, I would receive e-mails periodically from people proclaiming how they were going to return to Evan Roberts' home church (the Moriah Calvinistic Methodist Church in Loghour) and "re-dig the wells of revival." Simply put, this is spiritual nonsense. In the present day spiritual contest for revival and spiritual awakening, one can no more "re-dig the wells of revival" to achieve spiritual victory than one could raise the Arizona and send it into battle today to win the war against terrorism. The Arizona, along with the Missouri and the Bowfin, represent our history and our heritage, but neither represent nor can make a meaningful contribution to our destiny, except for the lessons which they embody. And that is the purpose of a memorial - to remind and to teach.

Conclusion

O.K., time to wrap this up. Like generals accused of building present plans around the last war, much of the church is looking to past awakenings and past structures for the future, as if history and heritage are our destiny. But just as the era of the battleship is over, Frost and Hirsch argue that the day of institutional Christendom is also over. It represents our history

Chapter 12 - House Church Reflections

and our heritage, but not our destiny. In the spiritual battle of our age, and the spiritual awakening which is unfolding, the River of God's Spirit is going to flow, not from old wells which have been re-dug, but through new channels like simple house churches which He is sovereignly raising up. New vessels to reach a new generation. God's will along with our spiritual destiny is always ahead of us, never behind us. It is time to leave the old wells behind, to move beyond the memorial stones of past battles, and to cross over into the new thing God has for us. The River of God is looking for new vessels to fill. Are you and the simple church in your house a vessel He can use?

He is coming. Are we ready? Is your House Church a channel through which He can flow?

 Let the River flow!

Preparing For A Spiritual Outpouring

Editor's Note: *Those of you who have regularly endured these e-letters will be aware of the profound experience which I related in my May 2, 2007 newsletter (which you can find starting on page 87). Since that "encounter" I have wrestled with how to adequately relate to you and to others the nature and the importance of the three words or "planks" which emerged from that experience (holiness/fear of the Lord, repentance & intimacy). This week's newsletter is another attempt on my part to further explore one of those planks, namely, holiness or "the fear of the Lord". Time (and your responses) will tell whether or not I've been successful.*

What Tozer Knew And Uzziah Forgot

King Uzziah of Judah had a problem that A.W. Tozer understood. It is a problem shared by the church in our time, including those of us in the simple church/ house church movement. And therein lies our story. In order to tell this story and properly frame it for our discussion, I want to share an extended passage from one of my favorite authors, A.W. Tozer. Recently, while rummaging through boxes of books left unpacked from our recent move, I came across his book, ***"Knowledge of the Holy"***. I hadn't read it in years, but I felt impressed to set it aside for reading during my devotions. That decision resulted in this newsletter. The first chapter of this small but powerful volume is entitled, *"Why We Must Think Rightly About God."* What follows is my redacted version for this newsletter. Here is what Tozer wrote:

"What comes into our minds when we think about God is the most important thing about us. The history of mankind will probably show that no people has ever risen above its religion, and man's spiritual history will positively demonstrate that no religion has ever been greater than its idea of God. Worship is pure or base as the worshiper entertains high or low thoughts

Preparing For A Spiritual Outpouring

of God. For this reason the gravest question before the Church is always God Himself, and the most portentous fact about any man is not what he at a given time may say or do, but what he in his deep heart conceives God to be like. We tend by a secret law of the soul to move toward our mental image of God. This is true not only of the individual Christian, but of the company of Christians that composes the Church. Always the most revealing thing about the Church is her idea of God, just as her most significant message is what she says about Him or leaves unsaid, for her silence is often more eloquent than her speech. She can never escape the self-disclosure of her witness concerning God . . . . A right conception of God is basic not only to systematic theology but to practical Christian living as well. It is to worship what the foundation is to the temple; where it is inadequate or out of plumb the whole structure must sooner or later collapse. I believe there is scarcely an error in doctrine or a failure in applying Christian ethics that cannot be traced finally to imperfect and ignoble thoughts about God . . . . It is my opinion that the Christian conception of God current in these middle years of the twentieth century is so decadent as to be utterly beneath the dignity of the Most High God and actually to constitute for professed believers something amounting to a moral calamity . . . . All the problems of heaven and earth, though they were to confront us together and at once, would be nothing compared with the overwhelming problem of God: That He is; what He is like; and what we as moral beings must do about Him . . . . The man who comes to a right belief about God is relieved of ten thousand temporal problems, for he sees at once that these have to do with matters which at the most cannot concern him for very long; but even if the multiple burdens of time may be lifted from him, the one mighty single burden of eternity begins to press down upon him with a weight more crushing than all the woes of the world piled one upon another. That mighty burden is his obligation to God . . . . The gospel can lift this destroying burden from the mind, give beauty for ashes, and the garment of praise for the spirit of heaviness. But unless the weight of the burden is felt the gospel can mean nothing to the man; and until he sees a vision of God high and lifted up, there will be no woe and no burden. Low views of God destroy the gospel for all who hold

Chapter 13 - The Fear of the Lord - Part 1

them. Among the sins to which the human heart is prone, hardly any other is more hateful to God than idolatry, for idolatry is at bottom a libel on His character. The idolatrous heart assumes that God is other than He is - in itself a monstrous sin - and substitutes for the true God one made after its own likeness . . . . Let us beware lest we in our pride accept the erroneous notion that idolatry consists only in kneeling before visible objects of adoration, and that civilized peoples are therefore free from it. The essence of idolatry is the entertainment of thoughts about God that are unworthy of Him. It begins in the mind and may be present where no overt act of worship has taken place . . . . Wrong ideas about God are not only the fountain from which the polluted waters of idolatry flow; they are themselves idolatrous. The idolater simply imagines things about God and acts as if they were true . . . . Perverted notions about God soon rot the religion in which they appear. The long career of Israel demonstrates this clearly enough, and the history of the Church confirms it. So necessary to the Church is a lofty concept of God that when that concept in any measure declines, the Church with her worship and her moral standards declines along with it. The first step down for any church is taken when it surrenders its high opinion of God . . . . Before the Christian Church goes into eclipse anywhere there must first be a corrupting of her simple basic theology. She simply gets a wrong answer to the question, "What is God like?" and goes on from there. Though she may continue to cling to a sound nominal creed, her practical working creed has become false. The masses of her adherents come to believe that God is different from what He actually is; and that is heresy of the most insidious and deadly kind . . . . The heaviest obligation lying upon the Christian Church today is to purify and elevate her concept of God until it is once more worthy of Him - and of her. In all her prayers and labors this should have first place. We do the greatest service to the next generation of Christians by passing on to them undimmed and undiminished that noble concept of God which we received from our Hebrew and Christian fathers of generations past. This will prove of greater value to them than anything that art or science can devise."

Preparing For A Spiritual Outpouring

How Uzziah Thought Wrongly About God

The story of King Uzziah's life is found in the book of 2 Chronicles, Chapter 26. What follows is not a detailed exposition of this chapter. Rather, the following represents my observations in light of the topic of the fear of God and thinking right thoughts about Him.

"Uzziah was sixteen years old when he became king, and he reigned fifty-two years in Jerusalem; and his mother's name was Jechiliah of Jerusalem. And he did right in the sight of the Lord according to all that his father Amaziah had done. And he continued to seek God in the days of Zechariah, who had understanding through the vision of God; and as long as he sought the Lord, God prospered him." (26:3-5)

Observation # 1: God genuinely prospers those who seek Him. The challenge here is that we don't get to define what "prosper" means. God does. The proponents of "the prosperity gospel" have usurped the conversation and have defined "prosper" in terms of material and financial prosperity. But success is always on God's terms, not ours. The roots of Uzziah's eventual downfall are found in his outward success. We assume that outward success is a sign of God's blessing. Yet, I have met very few people who learned important spiritual lessons from their success. When people are successful they usually don't' ask God *"Why did this happen to me?"* (A point made over a generation ago by G.K. Chesterton in "Orthodoxy"). Most important life lessons are learned from our failures, because failure has a tendency to drive us to our knees in search of both answers and mercy. Don't misunderstand me at this point. Success is a wonderful blessing, but it is a poor teacher. And one of the ways we begin thinking wrong thoughts about God is by misinterpreting our own success.

"Moreover, Uzziah prepared for all the army shields, spears, helmets, body armor, bows and sling stones. And in Jerusalem he made engines of war invented by skillful men to be on the

towers and on the corners, for the purpose of shooting arrows and great stones. Hence his fame spread afar, for he was marvelously helped until he was strong." (26:14-15)

Observation # 2: God loves to help the weak who seek Him, until they become strong. If you're feeling weak right now, there's good news: God loves to help the weak. But if you're feeling strong, I've got some bad news. God may not be in it. One of the ways we begin thinking wrong thoughts about God is by listening to and believing our own publicity. Our "fame" goes to our head and we begin thinking less about God's greatness and more about our own blessing. We still do lip service to God as the source of our blessing, but it is a hollow refrain. The awful reality is that we have come to think too much of ourselves and our "gifts" while thinking too little about God and His holiness.

"But when he became strong, his heart was so proud that he acted corruptly, and he was unfaithful to the Lord his God, for he entered the temple of the Lord to burn incense on the altar of incense" (26:16)

Observation # 3: Pride will turn your greatest strength into your greatest weakness, and your greatest blessing into your greatest curse. By now it was obvious that Uzziah was both strong and blessed. And that was the beginning of wrong thinking about God. Strength and blessing can do strange things to people. Together they become fertilizer for the weeds of pride. Uzziah had been so successful as King, his pride told him there was no reason why he couldn't be a great priest too! Uzziah made a mistake that is common among gifted people: He confused God's blessing with God's approval. And one of the ways we begin thinking wrong thoughts about God is by confusing His gifts and blessings in our lives with His approval of our beliefs, our opinions and our lifestyles.

"Then Azariah the priest entered after him and with him eighty priests of the Lord, valiant men. And they opposed Uzziah the king and said to him, 'It is not for you, Uzziah, to burn incense

to the Lord, but for the priests, the sons of Aaron who are consecrated to burn incense. Get out of the sanctuary, for you have been unfaithful, and will have no honor from the Lord God.' But Uzziah, with a censer in his hand for burning incense, was enraged; and while he was enraged with the priests, the leprosy broke out on his forehead before the priests in the house of the Lord, beside the altar of incense." (26:17-19)

Observation # 4: Pride causes us to forget who God is, who we are in relation to Him, and what He has called us to do. Uzziah was called to be King; He wasn't called to be a priest. Strength and blessing combined with pride to create wrong thoughts about God. Strength and blessing combined with pride to cause Uzziah to forget who he was, who God was, and what he had been called to do. Wrong thoughts about God will result in a wrong understanding of who we are in relation to Him. When we forget God's place, we quickly become confused about our own place.

"And Azariah the chief priest and all the priests looked at him, and behold, he was leprous on his forehead; and they hurried him out of there, and he himself also hastened to get out because the Lord had smitten him. And King Uzziah was a leper to the day of his death; and he lived in a separate house, being a leper, for he was cut off from the house of the Lord. And Jotham his son was over the king's house judging the people of the land." (26:20-21)

Observation # 5: King Uzziah received a rude awakening and a costly lesson regarding the fear of the Lord. The text tells us that Uzziah "hastened to get out because the Lord had smitten him." My impression is that Uzziah was smitten not only with leprosy, but with fear - the fear of God which results from a personal confrontation with His Holiness. The fear of God reminds us of who God is - a holy God who is not to be trifled with - and who we are in relation to Him - servants called to holiness and obedience. The fear of God breaks our pride and places us in right relationship to God and to the world around us. The fear of God restores God to His proper place, restores

Chapter 13 - The Fear of the Lord - Part 1

us to our proper place and causes us to once again think rightly about ourselves, about God, and about His purposes in the world. All of this happened to King Uzziah in a moment of time. And it cost him dearly, *"And King Uzziah was a leper to the day of his death; and he lived in a separate house, being a leper, for he was cut off from the house of the Lord."*

Tozer, Uzziah and House Church

O.K., time to stop circling the airport and land this thing. Tozer was right, of course. The most important thing about any man or woman is what he or she thinks about God, because *"We tend by a secret law of the soul to move toward our mental image of God."* It was true of Uzziah, and it is true of us as well. This leads me to conclude that, like Uzziah, every one of us needs to know four things: 1) We need to know God for Who He is, not for who we imagine Him to be; 2) We need to know who we are in relation to this God; 3) We need to know what He has done for us; 4) We need to know what He is calling us to do. These four issues are at the heart of the Church in every generation, including ours and including simple church or house church. The answers to these four issues will determine the DNA of the simple church/house church movement for the next generation, so they are of more than mere passing interest. This helps me understand why God chose the "express delivery" method of communicating this message to us (see Chapter 10) and why He "interrupted" my vacation to re-emphasize it's importance (see Chapter 12).

Finally, what does Uzziah's experience have to do with Isaiah's experience? It was the life and lessons of Uzziah that formed the backdrop for what God was going to reveal to Isaiah. How do we know? Because Isaiah tells us so: *"In the year of King Uzziah's death, I saw the Lord . . ."*. Sometimes God uses the experience of others to open our eyes so that we can see.

The River of God's Spirit, the River of Exekiel 47, is preparing to flow in power and blessing the likes of which this generation has not seen before. And the "three planks" of the channel He

Preparing For A Spiritual Outpouring

is preparing consist of Holiness/Fear of God, Repentance and Intimacy. Are you and your simple house church part of His channel? Are you seeking Him for how He wants you to build with these three planks? He is preparing to bring His "available church" into an Isaiah 6 encounter with Himself that will shape the DNA of the simple church/house church movement for a generation. Are you "available" to hear what it is He wants to say?

He is coming. Are we ready? Is your House Church a channel through which He can flow?

 Let the River flow!

The Fear of The Lord - Part 2

First Published September 19, 2007

Editor's Note: *I began this two-part message in my e-letter for August 29 which is reproduced in the previous chapter. Those of you who have regularly endured these e-letters will be aware of the profound experience which I related in my May 2, 2007 newsletter. Since that "encounter" I have wrestled with how to adequately relate to you and to others the nature and the importance of the three words or "planks" which emerged from that experience (holiness/fear of the Lord, repentance & intimacy). This week's newsletter is another attempt on my part to further explore one of those planks, namely, holiness or "the fear of the Lord". Time (and your responses) will tell whether or not I've been successful.*

What Tozer Knew And Isaiah Experienced (Isaiah 6:1-8)

In part one of this message I quoted an extended passage from one of my favorite authors, A.W. Tozer. I feel that this quote is so pivotal to this message that, at the risk of boring you, I want to encourage you to take a moment to re-read that quote from my previous newsletter. Let me re-iterate Tozer's point. Make no mistake. The most important thing about any man or woman is what he or she thinks about God, because "We tend by a secret law of the soul to move toward our mental image of God." It was true of King Uzziah, it was true of the Prophet Isaiah, and it is true of us as well. As I have examined Isaiah 6:1-6 I have been struck by the reality that it clearly teaches us four things that each of us must know in order to truly walk, serve and minister in the Kingdom of God: 1) We need to know God for Who He is, not for who we imagine Him to be; 2) We need to know who we are in relation to this God; 3) We need to know what He has done for us; 4) We need to know what He is calling us to do. These four issues are at the heart of the Church in every generation, including ours and including simple church or house church. The answers to these four issues will determine the DNA of the simple church/house

Preparing For A Spiritual Outpouring

church movement for the next generation, so they are of more than mere passing interest. I do not claim any unique insights on this passage. Rather, I come to this passage as one working to come to terms with it's meaning and significance. Hence, what follows are my reflections:

1. Here's Who God Is (vs. 1-4)

In the year of King Uzziah,s death, I saw the Lord sitting on a throne, lofty and exalted, with the train of His robe filling the temple. Seraphim stood above Him, each having six wings; with two he covered his face, and with two he covered his feet, and with two he flew. And one called out to another and said, "Holy, Holy, Holy, is the Lord of hosts, The whole earth is full of His glory." And the foundations of the thresholds trembled at the voice of him who called out, while the temple was filling with smoke.

I would dare say that the vast majority of churches in the western world are led by teachers, in keeping with our overall "rationalistic" approach to faith. Teachers are one of the 5-fold giftings of Ephesians 4, which means they are important to the overall equipping and building up of the church. But the weakness of every 5-fold gift lies in the shadow of its strength. The weaknesses of a teacher is that they have never met a problem that couldn't be solved with more teaching. Unfortunately, this approach doesn't work. How do I know? After 35 years of teaching on biblical finances in the church, Christian giving as a percentage has fallen by 35% (yep, 1% each year). There is more teaching on biblical marriage today than at any time in the life of the church (a la *"Focus on the Family"* et al), yet our divorce rate is equal to that of the non-church world. Why? Because good teaching alone is inadequate to solve deeply rooted spiritual problems. The same could be said of the issue of holiness. You cannot teach your way into the holiness of God any more than you can teach your way into a loving marriage. It is relational, not educational. What we in the Church need today is not a study on holiness. What we need is a genuine encounter with a living, holy God

Chapter 14 - The Fear of the Lord - Part 2

before Whom even the angels cover their eyes and declare *"Holy, Holy, Holy, is the Lord of hosts, The whole earth is full of His glory."* That is what Isaiah needed. He needed to see God for Who He is, not for who Isaiah imagined Him to be. And that is what we need, too. In the absence of such an encounter men create pseudo-holiness by means of legalistic rules. Religious legalism is like the veil over Moses' face when the glory of God's presence began to fade. It is man's attempt to convince himself and others that the glory of God's Presence has not departed; that the fire of God's holiness remains when, in reality, the fire is gone and altar has gone cold.

2. Here's Who I Am (vs. 5)

Then I said, "Woe is me, for I am ruined! Because I am a man of unclean lips, And I live among a people of unclean lips; For my eyes have seen the King, the Lord of hosts."

I am bothered by a trend I see in the church among believers today. It is a trend of self-exaltation. I hear it expressed in phrases such as "we're kings" or "God is releasing kings". I am bothered for several reasons. *First*, it is unscriptural. No where in the New Testament are believers ever referred to as "kings," except in 1 Corinthians 4 where Paul is ridiculing the idea (basically, "I wish you were kings, because then we would be reigning with you!"). We are described as a "kingdom of priests", but never as kings. *Second*, Jesus impressed upon His disciples the importance not of ruling and reigning, but of serving. Consider this passage from Luke 17: *"Which of you, having a slave plowing or tending sheep, will say to him when he has come in from the field, 'Come immediately and sit down to eat'? But will he not say to him, 'Prepare something for me to eat, and properly clothe yourself and serve me while I eat and drink; and afterward you may eat and drink'? He does not thank the slave because he did the things which were commanded, does he? So you too, when you do all the things which are commanded you, say, 'We are unworthy slaves; we have done only that which we ought to have done."* (Luke 17:7-10) The word "slaves" in this passage is the Greek word _doulos_, the same word Paul used to describe himself repeatedly as as "bond servant of Christ Jesus" (see Romans 1:1; Titus 1:1). **Third**, I am bothered because in my limited experience of 36 years in the church I have found that Christians are at their best when serving, and at their worst when "ruling". **Fourth**, I am bothered because Jesus is our model, and He declared that He did not come to be served, but to serve, and to give His life a ransom for many. (Matthew 20:28)

So, who am I in relation to this passage from Isaiah? And who are you? We are sinners, saved by grace . . . and called to serve.

3. Here's What He Has Done For Me (vs. 6-7)

Then one of the seraphim flew to me, with a burning coal in his hand which he had taken from the altar with tongs. And he touched my mouth with it and said, "Behold, this has touched your lips; and your iniquity is taken away, and your sin is forgiven."

As Isaiah discovered, the holiness of God has an amazing effect upon us. It "clears the sinuses" (so to speak) and places everything in its proper perspective. This includes the reality that our sin and lack of holiness is so great that it requires a divine remedy; a supernatural act on God's part to deal with it and to rescue fallen mankind. The very One Whose holiness demands our judgment and condemnation is the One Who provides the remedy for our predicament. Scripture describes this divine solution with the use of imagery and metaphor: fire, burning coals, washings, "as far as the east is from the west," etc. But they all point to one thing: The God Whose holiness cries out for our condemnation has made it possible for our iniquity to be "taken away" and for our sins to be "forgiven." And all of this imagery points to one thing: What God Himself has accomplished on our behalf through the atoning death of His Son, Jesus.

Chapter 14 - The Fear of the Lord - Part 2

4. Here's What He's Calling Me To Do (vs. 8)

Then I heard the voice of the Lord, saying, "Whom shall I send, and who will go for Us?" Then I said, "Here am I. Send me!"

Having been a believer and in the church for some 36 years now, I have heard innumerable missions messages built around this verse. Such messages almost always close with an exhortation that we need to tell God to "send me". But to use this verse out of context is to rob the passage of its spiritual power. It wasn't until Isaiah saw God for Who He truly is in all of His "terrible holiness", understood who he was in relation to this God and what this God of Holiness had done for him, that Isaiah was in a mental and spiritual position to answer the call and to say "send me". It was an encounter with God's holiness, resulting in a genuine "fear of the Lord" that motivated Isaiah to "go". I find it both interesting and instructive that this was the Apostle Paul's motivation as well: *"Therefore, knowing the fear of the Lord, we persuade men . . . ."* (2 Corinthians 5:11). Holiness and the fear of the Lord motivate people to a life of obedience and service in a way that no amount of teaching or cajoling ever could. No amount of teaching can produce this kind of obedience. It cannot be taught. It must be caught. And fire doesn't respond well to teaching; but it is always in search of dry kindling.

And this brings us to the simple church/house church movement. One of my greatest fears is that the simple church or house church movement will become co-opted by teachers who reduce it to a book writing, conference holding, note taking, notebook producing movement that seeks to offer *"Fire Building 101"* courses taught by people with no burns (if you missed the subtlty of that one, let me know and I'll 'splain it to you). I suspect that this is the Lord's "fear" as well, hence, the "three planks" He gave us (again, see Chapter 10). Again, let me be clear. We cannot teach our way into the kind of simple church/house church movement God wants to unleash. What is needed in the house church movement today is a band of believers who have had an Isaiah 6 encounter with the holiness of God and are prepared to say, like Isaiah, "Here am I, Lord. Send me."

The River of God's Spirit, the River of Exekiel 47, is preparing to flow in power and blessing the likes of which this generation has not seen before. And the "three planks" of the channel He is preparing consist of Holiness/Fear of God, Repentance and Intimacy. Are you and your simple house church part of His channel? Are you seeking Him for how He wants you to build with these three planks? He is preparing to bring His "available church" into an Isaiah 6 encounter with Himself that will shape the DNA of the simple church/house church movement for a generation. Are you "available" to hear what it is He wants to say?

He is coming. Are we ready? Is your House Church a channel through which He can flow?

 Let the River flow!

Money, Holiness, Power & Choices
First Published April 16, 2008

15

Prelude To What's Coming

Not too long ago in this political season I watched conservative commentator Pat Buchanan on *"Hardball"* with Chris Matthews. Chris Matthews (who makes Hammy the Squirrel from "Over The Hedge" look & sound tame) put Buchanan on the spot, and it went something like this: **Matthews:** *"So, Pat, I'm Thomas Torquemada (the Grand Inquisitor of the Spanish Inquisition) and I've got you on the torture rack and I'm turning the screws. You have to make a choice. Hillary or Obama. Which will it be? What's your choice?!"* **Buchanan:** *"What's my choice? I say, 'Keep turning the screws'!"*. Now that's funny! O.K., what's all this got to do with house church, you ask? Good question, Grasshopper. Nothing, actually. But it does highlight how difficult some choices can be. And that's what I want to talk about: the difficult choice which is about to confront the house church movement.

Those of you who are regular long-time victims, er, readers of this newsletter already know some of my thoughts on what I regard as the coming spiritual outpouring. Based upon recent events it is my personal conviction that we are now within weeks of seeing the beginning of an historic move of God. I do not base that on what I call "echo prophecies," echoing what other people may be saying. I attempt to block out that chorus of echoes, get alone with God and simply ask the question, *"What are You doing, and what do You want us to do in response?"* Based upon what I have heard and am now hearing, I believe we are on the eve of the greatest spiritual outpouring of the past 100 years. Could I be wrong? Of course. Only time will tell for certain. But this newsletter is my latest installment in a series of newsletters dating back to January of 2003 in which I have sought to articulate what I believe the Holy Spirit is saying about this coming move. Simply put, I believe the River of God's Spirit, the River of Ezekiel 47 is about to flow in unimaginable power and blessing, and I believe His chosen channel for this Season is the organic, simple house church

Preparing For A Spiritual Outpouring

movement. Furthermore, I believe that it is in preparation for that Outpouring that He is laying before His people some profound choices which will radically alter and shape both the Outpouring and the vessels.

Two Spiritual Battles

That's the background. Here's what I am sensing now. Over the past several weeks I've found myself fighting several spiritual battles. I won't bore you with most of them, save two. **First**, at the end of last month my wife and I were having coffee together in my "office" *(The Service Station* in north Spokane) on a Sunday morning (worshiping in the "First Church of The Holy Coffee Bean") with a mature prophetic person in our house church. In the midst of our conversation Randy turned to me and said, *"Hmmm, I'm sensing that this next month is going to be a tough month for you guys financially."* My first response was to mutter *"false prophet - that's the caffeine talking"*. But now that we are mid-way through that prophesied month (and, yes, things are brutally tight) I can honestly say that he was right on. As my wife and I reflected on what God is doing through this, I noted to her, *"This isn't about money. We've seen enough of God's miraculous provision over the past year that we know He can provide. So it isn't about the money. It's about something else. What is it about us that He's working to change?"* As this coming move unfolds I am personally reminded that God is more concerned with our character than He is with our comfort; and it is more often the case that our character and faith are built through seasons of need than through seasons of prosperity.

The **second** spiritual battle relating to this approaching season of visitation also unfolded this month. For the past couple of weeks I have sensed and have wrestled with a powerful "spirit of uncleanness" (as Dr. Phil would say, *"You either get it or you don't"*). It has been both intense and, well, nasty. Finally, this week, after I returned home from an evening outreach, I collapsed into a chair with my Bible and began crying out to God for insight into what this is all about. He led me back to a

Chapter 15 - Money, Holiness, Power & Choices

familiar passage in Isaiah Chapter 6. As I re-read that familiar passage I noticed something new that I hadn't paid attention to before. Note verse 5: *"Then I said, 'Woe is me for I am ruined! Because I am a man of unclean lips, and I live among a people of unclean lips; for my eyes have seen the King, the Lord of hosts.'"* Spiritual "uncleanness" is not new, but it does get powerfully revealed when God begins to move. I have written elsewhere (see Chapter 11, page 87) that in this coming move I believe God wants to bring His church into an Isaiah 6 experience of His holiness. Why? Because, as I understood in a fresh way this week, God wants a "clean" church, a "clean" vessel through which to flow. But just as Isaiah saw 2,600 years ago, the people of God today are "unclean". We are "unclean" people, and we dwell among other "unclean" people. It took me two full weeks of wrestling and harassment with an "unclean spirit" to finally understand what is happening. The three DNA markers of this coming move are going to be 1) Holiness & the fear of God, 2) Repentance, and 3) Intimacy. The first two of these address the issue of becoming a "clean" vessel through which the River of God can flow. The third represents the result of the first two. Holiness & repentance lay the foundation for genuine intimacy with God. They always have, and today is no different.

Making Choices

O.K., by now you may be saying to yourself, *"This newsletter has more loose threads than a cheap Mexican blanket"*. So let me see if I can now tie it all together. As this coming Spiritual Outpouring approaches, an Outpouring which I believe is going to transform the simple house church movement into a genuine vessel of God's Presence and Power, God is confronting us with some basic choices. The ***first basic choice*** is going to be a choice between money & holiness. Please hear me clearly: In the Kingdom of God, it's never about money. It's always about what God is seeking to accomplish in our lives - what godly Christ-like character quality He is working to build in us. Why? Because He knows better than we do that ***we will destroy with our character what we build with our gifts***.

Preparing For A Spiritual Outpouring

Allow me to give a recent, heart breaking example.

My friend Doug recently returned from a trip to Maui (where his family lives and does property development). While there he was invited to attend the "Maui School of Supernatural Ministry" at a local community center. It seems that the person leading the "school" had bought a complete set of DVDs which entitled him to show the DVDs and offer his own "School of Supernatural Ministry" at which you too could learn how to do "supernatural ministry." The DVDs were produced by a church in California which licenses the schools and the DVDs. And all for only $6,995.00! O.K. excuse me while I take my gloves off for a moment. First, if you genuinely think that you can receive divine anointing & power for supernatural ministry from a set of overpriced (and poorly produced DVDs) then I've got an old "Reverend Ike prayer cloth" I'd like to send you. You can have it for free, and I can assure you that it has at least as much "anointing" left in it as those DVDs you want to buy. Second, if you can fleece God's people for $6,995.00 in exchange for $100 worth of DVDs & packaging and then talk with a straight face about how God is "blessing" your ministry, then you have already made your choice between holiness and money . . . and I fear for you in this coming move. You are about to destroy with your character whatever you had hoped to build with your gift.

The Choice Between Power And Holiness

This example also serves to illustrate the *second* choice God is placing before His people in this coming move; the choice between power & holiness. There is a great deal of talk today about an outpouring of "spiritual power" in the last days. Most talk about any coming revival seems to quickly gravitate toward prophecies of "great spiritual power" manifesting in miracles, signs & wonders, etc, etc, etc. Allow me to offer a different scenario. God's primary desire in the coming Spiritual outpouring is NOT for a powerful church, but for a holy and repentant one. Toward this end God is offering His people a choice: Choose and seek "spiritual power" and the result will be

Chapter 15 - Money, Holiness, Power & Choices

"false fire" and "fire on ice" (like overpriced DVDs promising to turn your community center into a "school of supernatural ministry"). Choose holiness & fear, repentance & intimacy and you will, in fact, experience God's supernatural power in ways that will take your breath away. But it will be on His terms. Not yours.

Choices are not new to the organic house church movement. In a very real sense, involvement in the organic, simple house church movement has always been about choices.

One of **the first choice** those of us in this movement have made is a choice regarding the structure of how we do church. We have chosen a different structure that is less institutional and more organic. Church isn't about buildings, programs or structure. Genuine church or "ekklesia" can happen anywhere and is not structure-dependent. But merely changing the structure (or location) of where and how we meet isn't enough.

The second choice which normally faces organic church people involves "structure" versus "values". Structure is often the expression of a value, and your values will eventually shape your structure. To paraphrase Winston Churchill, we begin by shaping our buildings, but eventually our buildings shape us. Changing a structure without changing the underlying values which gave rise to that structure will create an inevitable tension that must eventually be resolved. Often that resolution is a "Honey, I shrunk the church" moment in which we realize that we are simply doing big institutional church in a smaller box. In our new house church equipping book, **"You Wanna Do What In Your House?!"** we list and compare 15 "Values" which distinguish simple house churches from traditional institutional churches (See *"Question 8: Hey, What's So Special About Meeting In Houses, Anyway?"*).

But let's assume for now that you have successfully confronted these first two choices. You've changed your structure, and you have been able to articulate your new organic church values. You are meeting regularly. Things are going well. Prayer &

Preparing For A Spiritual Outpouring

worship are going well, spiritual gifts are beginning to come forward and you are ministering to one another. There's even some growth taking place. You're actually beginning to look and feel like a 1 Corinthians 14 house church gathering. The good news is that you've come a long way. But the challenge is that you still have *a third critical choice* yet to make if you want to become that vessel, that channel, through which the River of God's Spirit can flow unimpeded in this coming move. It isn't my place to tell you how to make this choice. That's between you and God. He will carefully design and engineer the time, place and circumstance which will confront you with this critical choices between money, power and holiness. And as the old knight in *"The Last Crusade"* said to Indiana Jones: "Choose wisely".

He is coming. Are we ready? Is your House Church a channel through which He can flow?

 Let the River flow!

Bronze Serpents, Revival and The Lakeland Phenomenon

16

First Published May 28, 2008

My Experience With Golden Calves (And Bronze Serpents)

This calls for a story. Years ago my wife and I were both on staff with Campus Crusade for Christ (that's where we met). I had been involved with the local Crusade ministry at UNC-Chapel Hill, where I taught weekly LTC classes and assisted the local Campus Staff. In those days of the 1970s all Campus Staff had available to them a resource book officially known as the "Campus Crusade For Christ Campus Ministry Manual" (whether or not the beast still lives, I can't say). It was the size of large city phone directory. Between its covers was everything a good Campus Crusader needed for life and godliness. Need a ten week bible study? It's in there. Need the Four Spiritual Laws the size of an overhead transparency? It was in there. Need a six-month Leadership Training Class. It's in there. Need instructions on personal hygiene and the need to wear clean underwear. Yep, it was in there (No, I'm not kidding. Many people coming into the movement were coming out of the hippie counter-culture of the day and were in need of, well, a bath!). The "Campus Ministry Manual" was "the book" where you could find just about anything you needed to lead your ministry, all with officially approved forms. And the truly distinguishing characteristic of the manual was its bright goldenrod color (with appropriate black lettering), which almost predictably gave rise to its nickname among Campus Staff (drum roll please . . .) - "the Golden Calf".

O.K., at this point you're probably asking what this has to do with bronze serpents, revival and what's going on in Lakeland, Florida. Well, I've been asking myself the same question and, quite frankly, I haven't been able make the segue either. But I love the story and this just seemed like a good place to throw it in. But I promise that if a good segue comes to me later, I'll try to figure out a way to include it!. O.K., on to bronze serpents.

Preparing For A Spiritual Outpouring

The Last Thing God Did

Then they set out from Mount Hor by the way of the Red Sea, to go around the land of Edom; and the people became impatient because of the journey. And the people spoke against God and Moses, "Why have you brought us up out of Egypt to die in the wilderness? For there is no food and no water, and we loathe this miserable food." And the Lord sent fiery serpents among the people and they bit the people, so that many people of Israel died. So the people came to Moses and said, "We have sinned, because we have spoken against the Lord and you; intercede with the Lord, that He may remove the serpents from us." And Moses interceded for the people. Then the Lord said to Moses, "Make a fiery serpent, and set it on a standard; and it shall come about, that everyone who is bitten, when he looks at it, he shall live." And Moses made a bronze serpent and set it on the standard; and it came about, that if a serpent bit any man, when he looked to the bronze serpent, he lived. (Numbers 21:4-9)

I know you're familiar with the incident among God's people recorded in Numbers 21, but let me bore you with a quick summary anyway. God's people are wandering around in a wilderness of their own creation when they once again get "impatient" (any of this sound vaguely familiar?). They finally begin (once again) to whine and complain about the lack of accommodations, etc. God responds without warning by sending "fiery serpents" among the people who begin to die in significant numbers. The people repent and ask Moses to intervene and intercede with God. He instructs Moses to create an image of one of the serpents and to hoist it up on a pole for everyone to see. Whoever looks at the bronze serpent, though he was bitten, would live. It was an act of faith and obedience (and probably very "counter intuitive" - what good is looking at a snake on a pole going to do for a fatal snake bite?! Hello?!). Now, before leaving this passage I want to make just a couple of points. **First**, the serpents were the result of the people's impatience on the journey God had them on (Hmmmmmm). **Second,** while God used the bronze replica of the serpent to

Chapter 16 - Bronze Serpents

heal the people - in other words, it was "a God-thing" for that generation - He never used it again.

The Next Thing The People Did

O.K., 700 years have passed in the national experience of God's people when we read the following:

Now it came about in the third year of Hoshea, the son of Elah king of Israel, that Hezekiah the son of Ahaz king of Judah became king. He was twenty-five years old when he became king, and he reigned twenty-nine years in Jerusalem; and his mother's name was Abi the daughter of Zechariah. And he did right in the sight of the Lord, according to all that his father David had done. He removed the high places and broke down the sacred pillars and cut down the Asherah. He also broke in pieces the bronze serpent that Moses had made, for until those days the sons of Israel burned incense to it; and it was called Nehushtan. He trusted in the Lord, the God of Israel; so that after him there was none like him among all the kings of Judah, nor among those who were before him. For he clung to the Lord; he did not depart from following Him, but kept His commandments, which the Lord had commanded Moses. (2 Kings 18:1-6)

It is now the reign of King Hezekiah, one of the "good" kings of Judah. A national spiritual awakening is underway and Hezekiah is cleansing the land of idols. And one of the "idols" he must get rid of is the bronze serpent which has been preserved since the days of Moses. It has not simply been "preserved". It is now being worshiped: *"for until those days the sons of Israel burned incense to it"*. Offering incense to any image constitutes an act of worship, and that is idolatry in it's rawest form. But the people had found a way to "soften" their idolatry by referring to the object of their idolatry in dismissive terms. They called it "Nehushtan" which translates *"that bronze thing"*. It's nothing important, the people would say, *"its just that bronze thing"*. Funny how we find ways to minimize our idolatries, both then and now.

Preparing For A Spiritual Outpouring

God's Visitations And How Bronze Serpents Get Made

This weekend my wife and I took our young friend, Jaime, to see the new Narnia movie, "Prince Caspian". It's a good movie and I would encourage you to go. At one point toward the end, when the battle is intense, Lucy has an encounter with Aslan, the great lion. *"Why haven't you rushed in to save us, like last time,"* Lucy asks. *"Things don't happen the same way twice, dear one,"* Aslan replies.(Hmmm.) Military leaders are frequently accused of preparing to fight the last war instead of the next war. As Christians we are often guilty of idolizing the last move of God rather than repenting, seeking and preparing for the next move of God. But that's not how God works. Anytime God "touches down" in a "divine visitation" whether personally or corporately, there is a very real risk of that event becoming a Bronze Serpent to which we secretly begin offering incense, and which God must eventually break into pieces, because it has become an idol that He can no longer use. Revival isn't the result of a formula. It is the result of a personal visitation by a personal God, who always repeats Himself but never in the same way twice. But once God moves, we tend to turn His unique dealing into a formula or a Bronze Serpent.

My friend Wolfgang Simson likes to share what he calls his steps for turning any blessing into a curse. They run something like this (I'm sure Wolf will let me know if I get them wrong!):

Step 1: Someone has a blessed experience (like healing or "revival").

Step 2: Someone creates a story or testimony about their blessed experience (nothing like a youtube video!).

Step 3: Someone creates a methodology to instantly re-create that blessed experience (like an "impartation"?).

Step 4: Someone creates an institution or organization for the world wide marketing of that methodology (time to incorporate, copyright, trademark and produce some video training classes to sell on how you can do this too!)

Step 5: It becomes an institution (Wahoo!)

Step 6: Someone lays their hand upon the plow and looks back

Chapter 16 - Bronze Serpents

and disqualifies themselves for service in the Kingdom. In other words: it's over. We lay our hand upon the plow, but we look back at our Bronze Serpents and our idolatry disqualifies us for what God wants to do next.

Some of us are trying to lay our hand upon the plow of the new thing God wants to do, but we are looking back at our bronze serpent and insisting that God do it that way, rather than His way. That Bronze Serpent may represent what God did in the past (either personally or corporately), but it does NOT represent what He wants to do now & in the future. There are entire Christian organizations, ministries & denominations which have become bronze serpents. One of their primary purposes for existing is to memorialize what God once did, and to offer incense to a bronze serpent of God's past dealings. Whatever that Bronze Serpent might be in your own spiritual life, or in mine, it now represents the greatest barrier to us moving forward with God into the new season He wants to bring us into. I will dare to say that every one of us reading (or writing!) this newsletter has a bronze serpent in our lives that we need to give up and let God destroy in order to set us free for the new thing He wants to do in and through us in this upcoming move of God. What's the bronze serpent in your life? Deal with it . . . before God has to.

Bronze Serpents And Lakeland

If you haven't yet heard about what is occurring in Lakeland, Florida under the ministry of Todd Bentley, you probably soon will (if for no other reason than the PR machine is in high gear on this one). Let me begin saying that I find myself in the uncomfortable position of agreeing with J. Lee Grady, Editor of Charisma Magazine. I want to support and bless everything that God is doing, whether in Lakeland or anywhere else. My life's goal is not to ask God to bless what I am doing, but rather to find what God is already doing and blessing and to ask His permission to join in. In addition, as one who has dedicated himself to fasting and praying for a new spiritual outpouring for the past 12 years, I am keenly aware of the high level of

Preparing For A Spiritual Outpouring

expectation currently hovering over the Church regarding a coming spiritual outpouring. I share that sense of expectation. But I want it to be the "real deal" and not some bronze serpent that has been swept up into a worldwide PR machine of human invention.

I recently received the following e-mail from someone on this list. Please read carefully, and ask yourself if there is a "Bronze Serpent" here:

"If you have been following the teachings and prophecies of some of God's greatest men of our time, you may be aware that many feel that 2008 is a watershed year for the body of Christ. Bob Jones has been prophesying for over a decade that a great revival will begin in 2008. Paul Cain has had visions and dreams for over 30 years of a move of God that will fill stadiums with huge healing crusades all over America similar to but greater than the healing revivals of the early 1950's. He recently contacted Todd Bentley in Lakeland, Florida and told him that his revival there moving to the Lakeland Center is the beginning of the great revival. Bob Jones feels that this revival will result in the reaching of 1 billion souls for Christ before it is done! Rick Joyner received a word from God last year that if we would "Honor our Fathers" that God would send revival within 6 months. He took this to mean that we should honor the works and memories of the great healing evangelists of the 1940's and 1950's, even the ones that fell into sin. Not that we should ignore or excuse their sin, but that we should "cover" their sins with compassion like Noah's sons did when he was drunk and honor the good deeds they did without rehashing their failures. Rick Joyner feels that the revival will be in full swing by this fall."

Did you see it? Allow me. **First**, I have no doubt that the Israelites of Hezekiah's day felt that they too were simply "honoring the fathers" when they offered incense to "that bronze thing". I genuinely doubt that it ever occurred to most of them that they were practicing idolatry - worshiping some past thing God had done in the days of their fathers. "Honoring the fathers" can lead to bizarre things, even idolatry. **Second,** there

118

Chapter 16 - Bronze Serpents

has been a strong undercurrent for many years among Pentecostals to see a return of the Pentecostal healing crusades of the 1940s and 50s. Prophesying such a return has been a Pentecostal cottage industry for as long as I can remember. To me, in my limited perspective, it looks and sounds suspiciously like a bronze serpent - the worship and pursuit of what God once did, but not of what He intends to do. And I have discovered in my limited 37 years of Christian experience that God sometimes gives us what we ask for, because He knows that we are unable or unwilling to receive what He wants to give us.

Maurice's Observations

What follows are simply my personal observations, as a student of the history of revival, for what they are worth. I have not been to Lakeland, although I have watched some of the streaming video now available on numerous sites. I don't want to play "coy" so let me place my cards out on the table. If you haven't guessed already I think the Lakeland phenomenon (a better word at this point than "movement") is a bronze serpent, an effort to resurrect and promote an old move under the guise of a new move. Could I be wrong? Of course I could. That's why I want to offer the following observations.

1. Approaching God With Open Hearts. Whether Lakeland or any other phenomenon, we need to approach it and God with open hearts and open minds. I want everything God wants to offer His Church, even if it doesn't fit my preconceived paradigm of what I thought God might do. Otherwise I am simply attempting to fashion God and His dealings into my own image. May God keep us all open to every move of His Spirit, all the while discerning the gifts and distinguishing the various spirits.

2. "This" Versus "That". From all that I have seen and heard thus far (apart from the noise of the promotion and hype machine that is now in high gear), the Lakeland phenomenon appears to be a Pentecostal healing crusade on steroids.

Preparing For A Spiritual Outpouring

Numerous Pentecostal healing evangelists have been conducting such meetings for years. Benny Hinn has been filling arenas like the Lakeland Center for years with his healing crusades. Why were those NOT a new worldwide move of God but this one under Todd Bentley is? Hamilton Filmalter, a South African healing evangelist and acquaintance of mine, does evangelistic healing crusades in Pakistan with crowds numbering in the tens of thousands. The videos of his meetings with people being healed are more impressive than anything I have seen out of Lakeland. Why is that not the beginning of a worldwide move of God, but Lakeland is? The only difference I can see so far is that Bentley is part of a much better promotional network, including local "Impartation" meetings springing up around the country.

3. Anointing Versus Approval. Much has been made about Todd Bentley's eccentric behavior (tattoos, piercings, stage antics, etc.). My view is that God uses imperfect people simply because that's all the clay He has to work with (which means there is still hope for yours truly). But this raises a valid issue, namely, our tendency to mistake God's anointing for God's approval. God anoints His gifts in us because He graciously uses imperfect people - we hold His treasure in earthen vessels. Get over it. But when He chooses to do so we tend to mistake His anointing of His gift for His approval of our lifestyle. In other words, we tend to say: *"God is blessing my gift and anointing my ministry, so He must approve of all the things I do"* (lifestyle, dumb opinions, eccentric behavior, tattoos & piercings, lousy taste in music, stage antics, etc., etc.). Sorry, but NO! Never mistake God's anointing for God's approval. One is a manifestation of God's grace. The other is a manifestation of our character. And always remember that you will destroy with your character what you build with your gift. One of the greatest threats to any movement is the unconfronted and unhealed character flaws of it's leadership.

4. The Danger of "Pendulum Pushing". During the Welsh Revival of 1904 Evan Roberts observed that when there was a "lull" in the services, that's when people were tempted "to push

Chapter 16 - Bronze Serpents

the pendulum rather than raise the weights." (O.K., if you "technoweenies" are unfamiliar with weight-driven pendulum clocks then you probably missed the whole point, but I'll leave it to you to figure it out!). To update the metaphor, when things get quiet and there is a lull in the meeting, that's when people tend to turn up the volume on the sound system. In the absence of power, volume will do.

Ministries or movements which build themselves on "visions, signs and wonders" are uniquely susceptible to "pendulum pushing" by experience-oriented people who are always looking for "more". This is why people flock to meetings touting gold dust, gemstones, angelic visitations, etc. Bentley "pushes the pendulum" with talk of angelic visitations in his meetings. Quite frankly, we've had them too, but we do not spend time talking about them or using them to promote meetings. Besides, who do you want to guide your meetings; Jesus or an angel named "Emma" (tough call there, but I think I'm going to go with Jesus). In addition Bentley talks about having visited the "third heaven" where he met aborted babies who "need people to adopt them". The Apostle Paul visited the third heaven, too, but wasn't permitted to talk about what he saw there. Apparently, Bentley feels no such restriction. Sorry, but I trust Paul more than I do Todd. To me, this smacks loudly of "pendulum pushing" for all the wrong purposes. Beware meetings built on "pendulum pushing".

5. Collapsing of It's Own Weight. Call me foolish, but personally I believe that the Lakeland phenomenon will burn itself out and collapse under the weight of its own internal contradictions. I believe this to be the case based upon what I have shared above, and based upon what the prophetic people in our network have heard as they have prayed and sought God concerning it. As I was preparing this newsletter I briefly logged onto the official website of the sponsoring church just to see what was streaming at the time. What I caught was part of a message on how to "paydown an anointing". It was a message on money & giving from Malachi. The punchline was that you can "paydown" a spiritual outpouring by giving money to the

Preparing For A Spiritual Outpouring

ministry. In other words, God's spiritual outpouring & anointing can be bought. I offer that as just one example of the internal problems (and just plain ol' bad teaching) which will cause this phenomenon to collapse under it's own weight. What the prophetic people around me have heard is that this will come unraveled in anger and bitterness. I'm already beginning to understand why.

Where The River Flows From Here

As I have said in the recent past, I do believe we are on the eve of one of the greatest spiritual outpourings in the history of the Church, but Lakeland is not it. Rather, I believe it to be the distraction before the deluge. I believe we have heard clearly that the coming move of His Spirit will be characterized by three things: Holiness & the fear of God, genuine personal repentance, and intimacy. I would encourage you to pray for and to seek God for those three things as we move into this new season of His dealings.

He is coming. Are we ready? Is your House Church a channel through which He can flow?

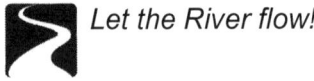 *Let the River flow!*

Holiness & Fear Revisited

First Published July 24, 2008

17

We live in a generation of believers who have lost their fear of God. Scripture has much to say about fear. Most Scriptural teaching on fear center's around God instructing His people not to fear people, events or circumstances. But Scripture recognizes and even commands, a good kind of fear, namely, the "fear of God". At the end of his search for wisdom the Preacher of Ecclesiastes (Solomon) declared, *"Now all has been heard; here is the conclusion of the matter: Fear God and keep his commandments, for this is the whole duty of man"* (Ecclesiastes 12:13). I would dare to say that our lack of fear toward God reflects our lack of understanding concerning His holiness. Holiness is that attribute of God's nature whereby He is totally and completely separated from sin and is singularly devoted to His own glory. Because we do not appreciate the Holiness of God, we do not fear Him in a genuine biblical sense. Isaiah rudely discovered this reality when he was confronted in the Temple by a vision of God in all His terrible holiness (Isaiah 6:ff). That encounter with God's holiness transformed Isaiah. And Isaiah discovered what David meant when he wrote under the inspiration of the Holy Spirit, *"The fear of the Lord is clean . . ."* (Psalm 19:9). The New Testament Church was rudely introduced to God's holiness in Acts Chapter 5 when He struck Ananias and Sapphira dead where they stood for the sin of intentionally lying to the Holy Spirit. The impact upon the Church of that encounter with God's holiness was profound: *"And great fear came upon the whole church, and upon all who heard of these things"* (Acts 5:11). God's holiness is not something to be trifled with.

Holiness is that penetrating light of God's presence which exposes our sin for the terrible rebellion and offense against God it truly is. How terrible is sin? So terrible that the wrath of God Himself is reserved for one thing and one thing only - the punishment of sin. God responds to sin as a personal affront to His holiness. So terrible is sin that it demands either the eternal punishment of the offender, or the substitute of a Savior sufficient to pay sin's price. The "fearfulness" of hell only makes sense in the blinding light of God's holiness. I do not believe that the biblical doctrine of eternal punishment in "hell" can be fully appreciated or understood apart from an understanding of God's holiness.

Ideas have consequences. And so does their loss. The present day loss of any genuine sense of God's holiness, and the biblical fear which accompanies it, has produced consequences in the life of God's people which are nothing short of catastrophic. The love of God has been distorted into little more than grand-fatherly sentimentality. The holiness, fear and wrath of God have been excluded from our vocabulary. Repentance has been forgotten while sin has been sanctified. The judgments of God have been muted and the Cross of Christ has been reduced to religious jewelry. Not only does this emasculated God want you to have your best life now, but he now promises that when you die, regardless of your condition, you will eventually end up in heaven, an uncomfortable citizen of a Kingdom whose motto is "holy to the Lord" (Zechariah 14:20). Richard Neibuhr summarized it in his classic observation:

"A God without wrath
brought men without sin
into a kingdom without judgment
through the ministrations of a Christ without a cross."

Discipline, Holiness & Healing

*"You have not yet resisted to the point of shedding blood in your striving against sin; and you have forgotten the exhortation which is addressed to you as sons, 'My son, do not regard lightly the **discipline** of the Lord, Nor faint when you are reproved by Him; For those whom the Lord loves He disciplines, And He scourges every son whom He receives.' It is for discipline that you endure; God deals with you as with sons; for what son is there whom his father does not discipline?*

Chapter 17 - Holiness & Fear Revisited

*But if you are without discipline, of which all have become partakers, then you are illegitimate children and not sons. Furthermore, we had earthly fathers to discipline us, and we respected them; shall we not much rather be subject to the Father of spirits, and live? For they disciplined us for a short time as seemed best to them, but He disciplines us for our good, that we may share His **holiness**. All discipline for the moment seems not to be joyful, but sorrowful; yet to those who have been trained by it, afterwards it yields the peaceful fruit of righteousness. Therefore, strengthen the hands that are weak and the knees that are feeble, and make straight paths for your feet, **so that** the limb which is lame may not be put out of joint, but rather be **healed**."* (Hebrews 12:4-13)

We could spend a great deal of time on this passage and still not exhaust it. Like all of Scripture, it is a pool that a child can wade in or that an elephant can swim in (No, that's not original. I borrowed if from Leon Morris and his commentary on the Gospel of John) But for now I want to highlight three words and their relationship to each other in this passage. Those words are "discipline," "holiness," and "healed". Let's begin with the word "discipline". The Greek word here is *paideia* which literally meant "tutorage" or "the education and training of a child" (the writer contrasts *paideia* with *nothos* which meant "bastard, illegitimate, counterfeit, or spurious"). By implication *paideia* could also mean "correction" or "punishment," but that was not it's primary or necessary meaning. It meant to tutor, train and educate a child. In case you missed the fine point here, we're the children and God is the parent. He is in the process of "tutoring" us in what it means to be a child of God. It is this process of "tutoring" which leads to the second word. The discipline or tutorage of God in our lives is both "good" (in and of itself) and is "for our good," even if the circumstances He uses to accomplish is discipline is not. If you have any doubt about this point, just re-read Job. The writer of Hebrews seemed to be addressing people much like you and me. Their tendency was to "lightly esteem" what God was doing in their lives. Another way of putting it is that they had a certain degree of contempt toward what was happening in their lives, and this

Preparing For A Spiritual Outpouring

presented a problem which called for strong language. Either recognize and submit to God's Fatherly discipline in your life, as any child should, or acknowledge that you are not a true child of God. Rather, you are an imposter, a counterfeit . . . even a "bastard" (ouch!).

The second word is "holiness" (*hagiotes*, from *hagios*, "holy"). The purpose of God's "discipline" or "tutorage" in our lives is so that we "may share his holiness". Holiness represents the very nature and character of God. It is that attribute and perfection of God's nature whereby He is uniquely separated from sin and wholly devoted to His own glory. It is not a list of rules or laws to be obeyed, but a nature and a character to be shared. We are to be "holy" because He is holy. And because, as Peter tells us, we have become partakers of the Divine Nature, we have been called to share this aspect of His nature & character. Hmmm. That's a big bone for us small dogs to chew on, so I'll leave you alone with it for just a moment.

The third word I want to mention is found in verse 13, "healed". The Greek word *iaomai* ("to heal or make whole") is used frequently in the New Testament for physical healing (see Matthew 8:13; 15:28; Mark 5:29; Luke 5:17; 6:19). While that seems to be the metaphor here, it raises some interesting thoughts. In some way that the writer of Hebrews does not explain or elaborate on, there seems to be a relationship between God's fatherly tutorage, sharing His holiness and healing. In the Greek text, verse 13 is constructed as a purpose clause: "strengthen the hands . . . and the knees . . . and make straight paths for your feet, so that (literally, "in order that") the limb which is lame may . . . be healed". This begs a question, namely, what does it mean to "strengthen and make straight" so that healing can occur? Within the context of the passage the answer would seem to be: submit to God's Fatherly discipline and pursue His holiness.

Holiness, Healing And The Kobayashi Maru

If you are a "Trekkie" then you will remember *"Star Trek II: The*

Chapter 17 - Holiness & Fear Revisited

Wrath of Khan." There is a scene early in the movie in which a group of Federation trainees are undergoing the "Kobayashi Maru". At first you think that the ship has been destroyed and the crew killed in an attack. Then you learn that it was only a training exercise - a simulated attack and an impossible situation in which there is no right or wrong answer. It is a test of character designed and intended to reveal the true character of those aspiring to leadership. Later in the movie you discover that young trainee James Kirk had "cheated" on the "Kobyashi Maru" test by reprogramming the computer to allow him a way to win. *"Received a commendation for original thinking"*, he boasted. Isn't that the American way - find a way to win, even if it means cheating?

Let me pose a question. Think of it as a "Kobayashi Maru" question. Suppose for just a moment that God the Father were to come to you and offer you a choice between sharing His Character (i.e., holiness) on the one hand, and experiencing His gifts (healing, signs & wonders, financial blessing . . . you know . . . all "the stuff". You fill in the blank) on the other hand. Which would you choose? Why? Like the "Kobayashi Maru" the offer and the question are a test of character, especially of those aspiring to leadership in God's Church.   And what if He were to tell you that it was an "either/or" choice for the rest of your life? Would you be willing to walk in His holiness & fear, repentance and intimacy for the rest of your Christian life, even if it meant you would never experience another miracle, sign or wonder? Like Daniel and his three friends before the fiery furnace, the test of genuine biblical character is the spiritual humility to pray for a miracle but the spiritual integrity and resolve to say "And If Not".

I'm Having De ja vu . . . Again

Our home church gathering last Friday evening turned interesting when, mid-way through our prayer and worship time, one of our prophetically gifted intercessors had a vision that our meeting was under demonic attack. We quickly dealt with the attack and returned to worship and prayer. A few minutes later this same intercessor said that the attack had subsided, and in its place there were three angels in our midst, attired in simple robes but covered with armor. She went on to say that they were there to deliver a single word: "Remember". Remember what? Their names said it all. The names of the three angels were: 1) Holiness/fear, 2) Repentance and 3) Intimacy (Then they were gone as quickly as they had come.) Does any of this ring a bell (See Chapter 10)?

Let me be blunt and get straight to the point. I believe that the Church in America is in the midst of a spiritual battle, a spiritual "Kobayashi Maru," if you will, that is confronting us with a test of spiritual integrity. It is a choice that we must make. On the one hand we are confronted with the Lakeland "phenomenon" and all of the extremism increasingly associated with it. On the other hand we have God calling His Church to remember and pursue holiness/fear, repentance and intimacy. And these two choices are, at this point in time, irreconcilable.

Make no mistake. The River of God's Spirit, the River of Ezekiel 47 is about to flow in immense power and blessing. But this River is going to flow through those channels where He is welcomed on the terms and conditions which He has set: holiness/fear, repentance and intimacy. Is your house church a vessel through which He can flow?

He is coming. Are we ready? Is your House Church a channel through which He can flow?

 Let the River flow!

Rent Heavens, Revival And House Church

18

Part 1 (Isaiah 63:15 - 19)
First Published September 17, 2008

Introduction

People who have stood in God's Presence (such as during times of genuine revival and spiritual outpouring) and who have touched and tasted the powers of the Age to Come often get "ruined" for life. What do I mean? Having drunk deeply at the well of the water of life, they find it difficult, even impossible to return to the days of artificially flavored soda pop. They have discovered the difference, and nothing less will do.

Such people also understand the meaning of genuine spiritual poverty. Having once swam in deep and great spiritual oceans they have become acutely sensitive to the changing of the tides. They know the difference between the high tide of spiritual abundance, and the low tide of spiritual poverty, for they have experienced both.

Isaiah was such a person. Early in His ministry, Isaiah had stood in the Temple in Jerusalem and had seen it fill with the very Presence of God. In that moment both Isaiah's life and his ministry were changed . . . forever. But years had passed since then. Now, at the end of His ministry, Isaiah knew that the spiritual tide had gone out in the life of the people of God. And we know this because Isaiah reflects upon the situation starting in verse 15 of Chapter 63, which is where we will begin.

Where Is God's Zeal & His Mighty Deeds?

"Look down from heaven, and see from Thy holy and glorious habitation; Where are Thy zeal and Thy mighty deeds?"

In this verse Isaiah openly wonders what has happened to God's zeal for His people. You see, Isaiah knew something about "the zeal of the Lord". In addition to standing in God's very Presence and personally witnessing and experiencing

Preparing For A Spiritual Outpouring

God's Holiness (see Isaiah Chapter 6), the prophet had personally witnessed God's "zeal" on behalf of His people in the incident with Sennacherib the Assyrian in Isaiah 37. When Sennacherib, King of Assyria beseiged Jerusalem and threatened to take the city, God spoke to Isaiah and promised that the City and it's people would be delivered:

"For out of Jerusalem shall go forth a remnant, and out of Mount Zion survivors. The zeal of the Lord of hosts shall perform this. Therefore, thus says the Lord concerning the king of Assyria, 'He shall not come to this city, or shoot an arrow there; neither shall he come before it with a shield, nor throw up a mound against it. By the way that he came, by the same he shall return, and he shall not come to this city,' declares the Lord. 'For I will defend this city to save it for My own sake and for My servant David's sake.'" (Isaiah 37:32-35)

Then, in a demonstration that the Kingdom of God consists not of words but of power, God in His "zeal" defended Jerusalem and His people and destroyed an Assyrian army of 185,000 in a single night: *"Then the angel of the Lord went out, and struck 185,000 in the camp of the Assyrians; and when men arose early in the morning, behold, all of these were dead."* (Isaiah 37:36)

Isaiah had personally witnessed God's holiness, God's zeal and His mighty deeds. He knew the difference between seeing them and not seeing them. And as he penned these words in Isaiah 63, he was not seeing them.

But Isaiah was more spiritually honest than we are today. He was willing to admit that the spiritual tide had gone out of God's people. And probably out of himself, as well. He was willing to openly admit his own spiritual poverty as well as the spiritual poverty of those around him. Are we? Verbiage about power is no substitute for power. Verbiage about healing is not substitute for healing. Verbiage about holiness, repentance and intimacy with God are no substitute for experiencing them and walking in them. The American Church talks a lot about such things, but

Chapter 18 - Rent Heavens

walks in precious little. Contrary to what Paul declares in 1 Corinthians 4:20, for most Western Churches and Western Christians, the Kingdom of God really does consist of words, rather than power.

When was the last time you candidly admitted your own spiritual poverty before the Lord? God loves it when we do. Through David he tells us that a broken spirit and a contrite heart He will not despise (Psalm 51). And Jesus Himself tells us that the "poor in spirit" are blessed in His sight. The recognition of our own spiritual poverty is a good thing, because when we are weak, then it is that we are truly strong. Scripture regularly warns and admonishes us that God is opposed to the proud (people who profess spiritual strength and blessing when the reality of their lives is something quite different). But He gives grace to the humble. Which are you?

Application: Honest Confession # 1: The Tide Has Gone Out of my Spiritual Life

Why Is God Restrained Toward Us?

The stirrings of Thy heart and Thy compassion are restrained toward me. For Thou art our Father, though Abraham does not know us, And Israel does not recognize us. Thou, O Lord, art our Father, Our Redeemer from of old is Thy name.

The admission of spiritual poverty is the first, and perhaps most important step, in coming to terms with what God is doing in our lives, or in the life of His Church. For Isaiah, the admission of spiritual poverty, the absence of God's "zeal" toward His people and the absence of His "mighty deeds" in their midst combined to signal a profound change in God's attitude toward His people and His dealings with them. Something had changed, and Isaiah knew it. God's attitude was different now than at previous times. He was no longer "stirred up" toward His people. A more literal rendering of Isaiah's words here would be, *"The commotion of your inmost parts and your womb of compassion are restrained toward me"*.

Preparing For A Spiritual Outpouring

If Isaiah were speaking today, many believers would want to comfort Isaiah by assuring Him that God's Presence never leaves us, or that God's love is always constant. But this kind of comfort would be little more than theological words spoken by people who have traded power for words, and whose own spiritual poverty has hardened into spiritual complacency. Such people have become satisfied with little, mistaking it for abundance. The self deception is made complete when we mask our poverty and our complacency with spiritual verbiage about "anointing" and "God's Presence". Isaiah was well aware that Jehovah was still his Father, *"Thou, O Lord, art our Father, our Redeemer of old."* But Isaiah understood things which we appear to have forgotten. He understood the changing of the spiritual tides. And he knew that something had changed in His relationship with God. The divine tide had receded and God was "restrained" in His dealings with His people. And this deeply troubled Isaiah. Does it trouble you in your own life? If not, isn't it time to ask yourself "Why?".

Application: Honest Confession # 2: Something Has Changed in My Walk with God and I Need to Set it Right.

Where Is The Fear of God?

Why, O Lord, dost Thou cause us to stray from Thy ways, And harden our heart from fearing Thee? Return for the sake of Thy servants, the tribes of Thy heritage.

The people of God had wandered away from God and His ways. In the process of wandering they had lost their fear of God. I've often wondered which comes first: Straying from God's ways or losing our fear of God. Isaiah doesn't address this question. He simply acknowledges the reality and seeks to deal with it. How does he deal with it? By asking God to return for the sake of His people. You would think at this point that Isaiah would call the people to repent. The Hebrew word translated "return" means "to turn" and is the word most frequently used for "repent". The idea is not a change of heart but a change of direction. But Isaiah doesn't call on God's

Chapter 18 - Rent Heavens

people to repent. Instead, Isaiah implores God to change direction and to come back to His people.

There's a point here. Restoring the fear of God to the people of God requires the work of God. We can't do it ourselves. Pursuing the fear of God without the Presence of God ultimately leads to legalism. And legalism always produces spiritual death. Recovering the fear of God requires a divine encounter. Isaiah understood this from personal experience, and so he implores God to *"return for the sake of Thy servants"*.

Application: *Honest Confession # 3: I've Lost the Fear of God and I Need to Seek God to Get it Back.*

Why Do We Look Like Everyone Else?

Thy holy people possessed Thy sanctuary for a little while, Our adversaries have trodden it down. We have become like those over whom Thou hast never ruled, Like those who were not called by Thy name."

When the tide of God's Presence recedes from His people, it soon becomes obvious, because the results are disastrous. And perhaps the most disastrous result is that the people of God soon begin to look no different than the surrounding culture. Listen to what Nehemiah told the people of God in his day when they wrestled with a similar problem: *"Again I said, 'The thing which you are doing is not good; should you not walk in the fear of our God because of the reproach of the nations, our enemies?'"* (Nehemiah 5:9). The people of God of Nehemiah's day had a two-fold problem. First, they had apparently lost their fear of God (when you're no longer walking in it, you've probably lost it). Second, the loss of the fear of God had led them to their next problem. You see, when we lose our fear of God we soon lose our holiness. And when we lose our holiness we lose that divine distinctiveness which sets us apart from the rest of our surrounding culture. Soon we begin to think, look and act like everyone else

Preparing For A Spiritual Outpouring

Application: *Honest Confession # 4: My Life Doesn't Look Any Different than My Unbelieving Friends.*

What Isaiah Understood

Americans are a "fix it" kind of people. Like the ancient Romans, we tend to be great builders, but lousy philosophers or theologians (when the Romans needed a philosopher they would simply go out and conquer another Greek city-state). If there is a spiritual problem, we want to write a book, create a DVD and offer a "three step plan" to fix it. It probably won't work, but as long as sales are good maybe no one will notice. But Isaiah saw things differently. Isaiah understood something we often forget. Isaiah understood that spiritual problems require divine solutions. And Isaiah understood that one of the first signs that God is about to move is the yearning felt and the groaning heard in the hearts of His people.

Throughout history the people of God have understood the significance of this spiritual yearning and groaning. *"This longing for revivals we cannot but consider a cheering indication of the noblest life. Next to a state of actual revival is the sense of its need, and the struggle to attain it at any sacrifice of treasure, toil or time."* (Minutes of the Presbyterian Church of 1857) A.W. Tozer understood this when he wrote that God is always "prevenient". Before a man (or woman) can truly seek God, God must first have sought the man. So it is with groaning. We yearn and groan for God because the Spirit of God groans in us and through us. And that means that God Himself is moving His people to ask for more.

So, What's All This Got To Do With House Church?

So, what's all this got to do with organic house church? In this coming move, God is looking for channels through which He can flow and vessels which He can fill. The greatest promise of organic house church is the potential and the promise it holds to become the new channel through which the River of God's Spirit can flow in this upcoming spiritual outpouring.

Chapter 18 - Rent Heavens

Conversely, the greatest threat to organic house church isn't heresy or divisiveness (yes, they're important, but the early church confronted and survived those threats and more, and we can too!). Rather, the greatest threat to organic house church is that it becomes "the new wineskin" while remaining devoid of any new wine. There's a word for a new wineskin without new wine: a "methodology". But I believe God has new wine for His new wineskin. I believe He is about to visit His Church and to permanently stamp it with three new DNA markers of His Presence and Power. The new house church wine of this coming move will consist of 1) a restoration of genuine holiness and the fear of God, 2) a restoration of a genuine spirit of personal repentance to believers, and 3) the restoration of genuine intimacy with God in His church.

He is coming. Are we ready? Is your House Church a channel through which He can flow?

 Let the River flow!

Preparing For A Spiritual Outpouring

Rent Heavens, Revival And House Church

19

Part 2 (Isaiah 64:1 - 12)
First Published October 1, 2008

"If one were asked to describe in a word the outstanding feature of those days, one would unhesitatingly reply that it was the universal, inescapable sense of the presence of God. Revival is the exact answer to such a sigh as that of Isaiah 64:1, 'Oh that Thou wouldst rend the heavens, that Thou wouldst come down, that the mountains might flow down at Thy presence." In 1904 the Lord had literally rent the heavens, and had scattered the satanic foes entrenched therein. The Lord had come down! The mountains were gloriously melted down in His presence." R.B. Jones on the Welsh Revival of 1904 in **"Rent Heavens"**

Introduction

Recent events in Lakeland, Florida have served to highlight the spiritual hunger of many people for a genuine divine encounter; a "visitation" that we commonly refer to as "revival". Those same events have also highlighted the need to return to a Scriptural understanding of what we mean by "revival". Scripture doesn't have a lot to say about "revival," at least not as an abstract concept to be debated. There are references to the need for individuals to be personally "revived," as in Psalms 85:6 where the Psalmist says, *"Wilt Thou not Thyself revive us again, that Thy people may rejoice in Thee?"* (See also, Psalm 138:7; Isaiah 57:15; Hosea 6:2). The prophet Habakkuk cried out for God to revive His work when he said, *"Lord, I have heard the report about Thee and I fear. O Lord, revive Thy work in the midst of the years, in the midst of the years make it known; in wrath remember mercy"* (Habakkuk 3:2). Rather than offering us an abstract or theoretical discussion about revival, Scripture simply gives us descriptive examples of times or seasons when God, in His mercy, has opened the heavens and touched His people.

Historians of revival tell us that every great spiritual outpouring of the last 300 years was preceded by a period of time during

Preparing For A Spiritual Outpouring

which two things took place. **First,** there was a period of time preceding the outpouring when the Church recognized and came to terms with the condition of it's own spiritual poverty. Writing of the time leading up to the Second Great Awakening (1799-1811), historian J. Edwin Orr observed,

"The new rationalism - like evangelicalism - claimed to be vitally interested in the welfare of man, equally ready to grant him liberty, equality and fraternity. Its greatest lack lay in its inability to satisfy him in the things of the spirit. It offered bread, but forgot that man could not live by bread alone. Its appeals were heeded, and the multitudes turned away from the things of the spirit. Evangelical Christians knew that they faced defeat. They began to pray the prayers of desperate men."

And this leads to the **second** thing that has always occurred prior to great spiritual outpourings. Desperate Christians began to humble themselves and to pray the prayers of desperate men. In last week's newsletter we looked at Isaiah 63:15-19 and saw how Isaiah acknowledged and understood the spiritual poverty of his own day. In Isaiah Chapter 64 we will see how Isaiah's spiritual poverty and desperation resulted in one of the greatest cries for revival and spiritual outpouring ever recorded in Scripture: *"Oh, that Thou wouldst rend the heavens and come down".*

I believe that we stand today on the verge of another such time and season of "rent heavens" when God is going to visit His people and transform the life of His Church (not to mention touching the unbelieving world with redeeming, healing and transforming power). The River of Ezekiel 47, the River of God's Spirit, is preparing to flow in power and blessing not seen in over a hundred years. The question that haunts me is simply this: Is the cup of our desperation, the cup which holds the desperate prayers of God's people, truly full to overflowing? As we seek God in preparation for this outpouring of the River of His Presence we would do well to take a fresh look at what the Scriptures teach us about such a time as this. With this in mind, I want to look at Isaiah 64:1-12.

Chapter 19 - Rent Heavens - Part 2

A Prayer of Longing For The Presence of God (64:1- 4)

Oh, that Thou wouldst rend the heavens and come down, That the mountains might quake at Thy presence — As fire kindles the brushwood, as fire causes water to boil — To make Thy name known to Thine adversaries, That the nations may tremble at Thy presence! When Thou didst awesome things which we did not expect, Thou didst come down, the mountains quaked at Thy presence. For from of old they have not heard nor perceived by ear, Neither has the eye seen a God besides Thee, Who acts in behalf of the one who waits for Him.

I understand that there are those of you who are far better at biblical exegesis than I will ever be. So please don't feel limited by my observations. I want to look at this section by asking a series of questions based upon what I see in the text.

1. Are we seeking God on His terms, or on our terms?
There is actually a whole series of questions that should probably be asked here. Such as, do you long for God's Presence? Isaiah did. Do we? I am amazed by the number of professing believers who show little or no interest in a divine visitation. But if you are longing for a divine visitation, what are you longing for? Do you want God to come and fix your problems (healing, finances, relationships, etc), or do you want God to come and glorify Himself at your expense? And through all of this, are you longing for God to come on His terms or on yours? Would you long for His visitation even if you knew that His Presence might consume you? The Prophet Isaiah, who had stood in God's presence and who understood the consuming nature of such a visitation, longs for God's Presence to come down among men. But Isaiah understood that when God's Presence comes, it comes like a consuming fire, "*As fire kindles the brushwood, as fire causes water to boil*." Isaiah understood what fire does - it burns, consumes and boils. Times of revival when the Presence of God comes upon people are often described as times of fire, which I believe speaks to us about the "consuming fire" of God's holiness.

Preparing For A Spiritual Outpouring

2. What's your purpose for desiring God's Presence: I'm personally concerned that there are too many bored believers today who are looking for a new "experience" that will make them "glow in the dark" and "wow" their friends. But the purpose expressed here by Isaiah for the fire of God's Presence causing the mountains to quake is *"to make Thy name known to Thine adversaries, that the nations might tremble at Thy presence."* God wants to come to us in a season of revival, in power and in fire, in order to heal and renew His Church and to empower it to reach the nations. Who do we want to reach? What's our purpose in seeking God's Presence in revival. Why do we want God to rend the heavens and come down? Is it simply to fix our problems and to make us feel good, or is it to see our homes and families healed so that we can reach our generation for Christ?

3. Are you seeking the God of your own expectations? I'm convinced that God loves surprises. God loves to come at a time of His sovereign choosing, when His adversaries least expect it and think that they have the upper hand. For this reason, there is an element of surprise to what God does in revival. God wants to do something awesome that we don't expect. Secular historians frequently criticize military planners for preparing to fight the last war, in other words, basing today's preparations upon the experience of the previous war they fought. The Church does the same thing. We are always trying to re-live or re-create the last great move of God in revival (as I stated in my article "Bronze Serpents, Revival & The Lakeland Phenomenon," for which I was roundly criticized - "ripped a new one" would be more accurate!) . We must not limit God either to the past - trying to re-live or re-create past revivals - or to our own personal experience. Isaiah warns us that in the coming move of God He is going to do things which are outside of the box of both your personal experience and your expectations of past revivals.

4. How long are you willing to wait upon God to act on our behalf? Americans are not good at waiting. We tend to be an "action" oriented people whose motto is *"Don't just stand there;*

Chapter 19 - Rent Heavens - Part 2

do something!" But the Kingdom of God often operates on the basis of different principles, such as waiting. On more than one occasion God has turned the American motto on its head by telling His people in times of crisis, *"Don't do something; just stand there!"* (See Exodus 14:13; 1 Samuel 12:16; 2 Chronicles 20:17). God often tells His people to simply "wait" upon Him. Most of us have never seen what God can truly do because we're unwilling to wait on Him long enough to find out. Now, I happen to believe in "active waiting." I believe that fasting, prayer and repentance are among God's appointed means whereby His people can actively wait upon Him, beseeching Him to act on our behalf. This kind of purposeful, active waiting upon God has two results. **First**, I believe it changes us, as we will see in verses 8 - 12 below. But, **secondly**, it gives God the freedom to work in such a way that He gets the glory, rather than us. Let me ask you something. If God were to bless all of your plans and activities, who would get the glory? You, or God?

In the late 1850s there was a powerful movement of God in revival which swept across America, starting in 1857. By 1859 it was also sweeping through the country of Wales, in the powerful Welsh revival of 1859. One of the men greatly used of God to lead thousands of people to faith in Christ was a Calvinistic Methodist pastor by the name of David Morgan. His traveling companion once related the following story about one of their preaching trips:

"The evening service was terrible. So near was the revivalist to his God, that his face shone like that of an angel, so that none could gaze steadfastly at him. Many of the hearers swooned. On the way home I dared not break the silence for miles. Towards midnight I ventured to say, 'Didn't we have blessed meetings, Mr. Morgan?' 'Yes,' he replied; and after a pause, added, 'The Lord would give us great things, if He could only trust us'. 'What do you mean?' I asked. 'If He could trust us not to steal the glory for ourselves.' Then the midnight air rang with his cry, at the top of his voice, 'Not unto us, O Lord, not unto us, but unto Thy name give glory'."

Preparing For A Spiritual Outpouring

I believe that God wants to use this season of preparation and waiting upon Him in humility and obedience for the purpose of raising up a generation of believers who have passed through the fire of His holiness and who can be trusted by the Holy Spirit with great endowment of power; trusted not to steal the glory that rightly belongs to God alone. As this passage tells us, I believe we have yet to see what God will do for a generation of believers who are willing to wait upon God to act on our behalf.

God's Presence Highlights Our Sinfulness (64:5 - 7)

"Thou dost meet him who rejoices in doing righteousness, Who remembers Thee in Thy ways. Behold, Thou wast angry, for we sinned, We continued in them a long time; And shall we be saved? For all of us have become like one who is unclean, And all our righteous deeds are like a filthy garment; And all of us wither like a leaf, And our iniquities, like the wind, take us away. And there is no one who calls on Thy name, Who arouses himself to take hold of Thee; For Thou hast hidden Thy face from us, And hast delivered us into the power of our iniquities."

Often times we do not fully comprehend what it is we are praying for. To pray for God's Presence is to invite a genuine encounter with His holiness. It should therefore come as no surprise that during times of revival, individuals are often dramatically forced to deal with their own sin. During such seasons of spiritual outpouring, when God's presence comes among His people in great power and holiness, something happens. Our sins are suddenly forced into the blinding light of His holiness. All of the sin and ugliness of our lives that we have been suppressing and ignoring is suddenly flushed to the surface as the Holy Spirit reveals and convicts us of sin and demands that we confess, repent and forsake. And it often feels like an inescapable consuming fire.

A powerful example of this comes to us from the Korean period of the Great Welsh Revival of 1904, during the winter of 1907. An Englishman, Lord William Cecil, was present during the

Chapter 19 - Rent Heavens - Part 2

"terrible" meeting that took place in the Central Presbyterian Church in Pyongyang. He was so excited and moved by what he witnessed that he did what an Englishman does when he gets excited; he wrote a letter to **The Times** of London, describing the scene:

". . . an elder arose and confessed a grudge against a missionary colleague and asked for forgiveness. The missionary stood to pray but reached only the address to Deity: 'Aboji!' 'Father!' when, with a rush, a power from without seemed to take hold of the meeting. The Europeans described its manifestations as terrifying. Nearly everyone present was seized with the most poignant sense of mental anguish; before each one, his sins seemed to be rising in condemnation of his life. Some were springing to their feet, and pleading for an opportunity to relieve their consciences by making their abasement known; and others were silent, but rent with agony, clenching their fists and striking their heads against the ground in the struggle to resist the Power that was forcing them painfully and agonizingly to confess their misdeeds."

Again, God rent the heavens, came down, and the fire of His Presence consumed all before it. The fire burned every night that week, until the Holy Fire of God's Presence had burned its way through the Church and the body of Christ had been cleansed. In the meetings that followed, conviction of sin and reconciliation of enemies took place on a wide scale. Not only was there deep confession of sin, but so much restitution took place that the local unbelieving Koreans were astounded and a powerful move of evangelism took place. Perhaps one of the reasons why the "unbelieving nations" don't tremble today is because they don't see the power and presence of God burning its way through the Church today. In this "season of desperation" as we fast and pray in preparation for the coming outpouring we need to ask God to visit us with His Presence, to reveal our sins in the light of His holiness, to deal with our sins in confession and repentance, so that He can truly empower us to be a light and a testimony which causes the nations to tremble at the greatness of our God.

Preparing For A Spiritual Outpouring

Are You Prepared For God To Re-Shape You? (64:8-12)

But now, O Lord, Thou art our Father, We are the clay, and Thou our potter; And all of us are the work of Thy hand. Do not be angry beyond measure, O Lord, Neither remember iniquity forever; Behold, look now, all of us are Thy people. Thy holy cities have become a wilderness, Zion has become a wilderness, Jerusalem a desolation. Our holy and beautiful house, Where our fathers praised Thee, Has been burned by fire; And all our precious things have become a ruin. Wilt Thou restrain Thyself at these things, O Lord? Wilt Thou keep silent and afflict us beyond measure?

The theme of this passage is found in verse 8, *"But now, O Lord, Thou art our Father, We are the clay, and Thou our potter; And all of us are the work of Thy hand."* When God rends the heavens and comes down in a season of genuine spiritual outpouring He initiates a process of personal transformation and re-shaping. He takes His people through the fire of His Presence; a fire that purifies us, consumes our sins and our failures, and enables Him to re-shape us, like a potter reshaping the clay and re-firing the vessel. The result is that He remakes us into vessels which He can use for His glory. Are you ready to give God permission to take the clay of your life, to place it on His potter's wheel and to remake you into the new person He wants you to be? If not, stop praying for God to "rend the heavens and come down," because, otherwise, you won't like what He has planned for you!

He is coming. Are we ready? Is your House Church a channel through which He can flow?

 Let the River flow!

The Anguish of Revival

First Published July 21, 2009

20

While others slept, he rose to pray. It was not the first time he had risen in the early morning hours to pray, nor would it be his last. The birth of a Church and the future of a nation demanded nothing less. So with only the stars and the angels as his witnesses, he wrestled with God over the future of his beloved but troubled nation. One of the sources of his nation's problems, Mary Queen of Scotland, had once remarked that she feared the prayers of this man more than she feared all the armies of Europe. If she could have witnessed his intercessions this night, her worst fears would have been confirmed, for here, alone beneath the stars, was a man who knew how to wrestle with God . . . and prevail. "Great God," cried John Knox, "Give me Scotland, or I shall die." The mantle of intercession that rested upon John Knox would one day be picked up and carried by his associate and son-in-law, John Welch, who married Knox's daughter, Elizabeth. Welch became widely known for his personal commitment to fasting and prayer, and for the significant amount of time he spent in personal prayer, often as much as eight hours a day. He also became known for the tremendous spiritual power which seemed the outward result of his fervent intercessions. On more than one occasion his wife, Elizabeth, would awaken to an empty bed and find her husband praying alone in the cold night air of their garden, praying "with great force & fervency, mixed and accompanied with floods of tears," crying out, "Lord, wilt Thou not grant me Scotland?" She would remember the times she had heard her father, John Knox, pray with a similar burden on his heart, "Great God, give me Scotland, or I shall die." And how many times had she heard her husband wonder aloud how a Christian could lie in bed all night never rising to watch and pray. Such are the wrestlings and intercessions of those whom God has used, and continues to use today, to bring revival and to change the course of nations and of history.

Welcome to "the anguish of revival". Readers of this weekly

Preparing For A Spiritual Outpouring

(well, occasionally weekly) missive are well aware of my personal belief in and commitment to a coming spiritual awakening.

Prophesying a coming spiritual awakening has become somewhat of a cottage industry in certain quarters of the church. But as I reflect upon much of the "revival chatter" today I am struck by something. Something that is lacking. Where is the deep personal anguish of soul over the condition of the Church and the state of the world? Where are the weeping prophets and apostles who are agonizing over the sin, rebellion, worldliness and lack of holiness and repentance among God's people. This point was recently brought home to me by a brief audio/video clip of a message by David Wilkerson. As I listened to it I found myself weeping and wondering how my own heart had become so callous. I remembered the season of fasting and prayer for revival that God had taken me through (1995-2007) and the prolonged times of intercession, frequently weeping and sobbing uncontrollably over what God revealed to me about His Church and His plans for revival. But that season of anointing lifted two years ago and since then, like Habakkuk, I have simply climbed into my watchtower to tremble, to wait and to watch for what God intends to do next . . . and to pray that God would continue to break my heart with the things that break His heart.

Every spiritual awakening of the past 500 years has been preceded by men and women of God who privately agonized and travailed in prayer over the state of the Church and the condition of God's people. They didn't "agonize" on stage to be seen. They agonized in private for an audience of One. Much of the "revival chatter" I hear today suggests that much of the Church is expecting the next spiritual awakening to be a huge divine "block party" complete with "Holy Spirit magic tricks" to entertain the kids. If that's your expectation as well, you might want to get prepared for a let down. The "clean" prophetic intercessors I have been communicating with are hearing something quite different. They are hearing such things as "judgment on the high places" and "tornadoes of destruction"

Chapter 20 - The Anguish of Revival

sweeping through the Church. What we are hearing is both blessing and judgment. And like Habakkuk, what I hear makes me tremble over what God is about to do.

So, what about you?

What are you agonizing over in your times of intercession. If you want some specific things to pray over concerning this coming season of revival, let me offer you four:

1. Pray for a renewed sense of the fear and the holiness of God. Pray over such passages as Isaiah 6:1-7 and Isaiah 64. In the coming move, anything that does not spring from the fear and holiness of God will be illegitimate and a deception.

2. Pray for a God-breathed spirit of personal repentance. Repentance has become "the lost heart" of the Church. God intends to restore it. He will restore it by re-introducing us to His fear and holiness. Isaiah's repentance in Isaiah 6 was the outflow of a genuine encounter with God and His holiness. I find this interesting because Isaiah was already a "prophet" who had walked with God - like many Christians today who have told me point-blank, "I don't have anything I need to repent of". Hmmm. Neither did Isaiah prior to Chapter 6. Funny how a genuine encounter with God in all His awesomeness changes our perspective on ourselves and the world around us.

3. Pray for a renewed intimacy with God. Isaiah's encounter with God's holiness led to personal repentance and cleansing. This in turn led to renewed intimacy - he heard God's voice more clearly than ever before saying, *"Whom shall I send, and who will go for us?"* Biblically speaking, any intimacy with God that is not founded upon His holiness and our repentance is false intimacy. And genuine intimacy with God leads to obedience.

4. Pray for how your obedience might express itself in reaching out to "the least of these". Yep, I'm back to that. I believe it is God's heart in this season. Read Matthew 25:31ff until that sinks in. And, yes, He's speaking to you. What are you going to do to make this real in your own life, and in the life of your house church.

5. Pray about how you are going to quickly equip those new people who come into your house church fellowship. How will you do it in such a way that they can duplicate and pass on to others in their own house churches what they have learned and experienced in yours. Are you simply a "small group leader" or the facilitator of a genuine 1 Corinthians 14 gathering of the ekklesia. Remember, we reproduce who we are, not what we teach; which is why the ability to model what genuine house church community looks and feels like is so important. You are the model others will reproduce

He is coming. Are we ready? Is your House Church a channel through which He can flow?

 Let the River flow!

A Bride Holy & Blameless, Without Spot or Wrinkle

21

First Published August 20, 2009

"But as the church is subject to Christ, so also the wives ought to be to their husbands in everything. Husbands, love your wives, just as Christ also loved the church and gave Himself up for her; that He might sanctify her, having cleansed her by the washing of water with the word, that He might present to Himself the church in all her glory, having no spot or wrinkle or any such thing; but that she should be holy and blameless." (Ephesians 5:24-27)

"Why are we not more holy", asked John Wesley. *"Because we are enthusiasts, seeking the ends without the means."*

I've lost track of the number of times I have heard a speaker (often in the context of revival and what God wants to do in a coming spiritual outpouring) allude to this passage by declaring that before Jesus returns He wants a bride that is holy and blameless, without any spot, wrinkle or blemish. What is nearly always left out of the conversation is any serious reflection on how God intends to bring this about. The hearer is left with the impression that God is going to wave His magic miracle wand over the Church and we will all wake up one day (much to our pleasant surprise) holy and blameless.

O.K., at the outset here I want to point out that this passage from Ephesians deals with two (2) forms of "sanctification". The first is what we would call "positional sanctification". This means that we (the Church "militant and universal") are ALREADY holy and blameless ("sanctified") by our position "in Christ", based upon His finished work of atonement and redemption and our faith in that finished work. The second form of sanctification is what Paul is urging the Ephesians on towards, namely, "experiential sanctification". This is the working out of our positional sanctification in our daily experience. You and I may enjoy "positional sanctification" with Christ, but let's face it, our lives are filled with "stuff" that needs to be confronted and dealt

Preparing For A Spiritual Outpouring

with. In other words, we all have spots, wrinkles and blemishes. Not to put too fine a point on things, but there is "sin in the camp"; both in your camp and in mine. And God wants to deal with it.

So, this brings us back to our original point. As part of an upcoming move of God's Spirit in awakening and revival, if God wants to produce a bride *"having no spot or wrinkle or any such thing"*, what exactly does that mean and what will that look like? As I have written previously, I believe it means that God intends to return genuine holiness to His Church; experiential holiness of the type that Isaiah experienced in Isaiah 6:1ff. Simply put, He wants a "holy" bride.

This, of course, begs for a question: *"What is holiness?"* And here is my answer: Holiness is that perfection of God's nature whereby He is totally and completely separated from sin and is singularly devoted to His own glory. I see two things in this definition. *First*, I see a "separation" from sin. *Second*, I see a "devotion" to God and His glory.

Separation. The command of Scripture is clear (yep, even in the Greek). We are to be holy, just as God is holy. This means the same for us as it does for God Himself, namely, it means "separation". It means that we must deal with sin in our lives. The ideas of "spots, wrinkles and blemishes" are simply metaphors for sin. God wants a bride that has separated herself from sin. He wants holiness among His people. To say that God wants holiness among His people is to say that God is after our character. I hear a lot of talk today about how the coming move of God is going to be about miraculous signs and wonders on an unprecedented scale. I believe this to be both true and false. I am convinced that in this coming move of God's Spirit, character - holiness - trumps power. Read that sentence again . . . and again, until it sinks in. While it is true that God can make a donkey talk and prophesy (usually an argument for how God uses fallen people in spite of their character issues), there is a profound difference between a believer and a donkey. The donkey will never know holiness, never partake of the divine nature and never experience the spiritual transformation of Christ-likeness. In other words, the donkey has no hope or expectation of its character ever matching its "gifting". Why, then, would we want to breed more such hopeless creatures? And why would we encourage more prophesying donkeys in the Church. Are you prepared for God to go after your character? Are you prepared for the Holy Spirit to shine the searching light of God's presence into the darkest recesses of your soul and to show you things you had hoped to never see? Are you prepared for the "separation" of holiness?

Devotion. What are you devoted to? People? Family? Programs? Career? Education? Hobbies? Make you own list and then ask yourself a simple question: Where does God and His glory fit on your list? Jesus expressed His own devotion to God's glory by declaring that He only did that which He saw the Father doing, and only spoke that which He heard the Father saying. Is that true of us? Jesus also expressed His true devotion to the Father when He declared, *"'Father, glorify Thy name.' There came therefore a voice out of heaven: 'I have both glorified it, and will glorify it again'"* (John12:28). Jesus' devotion to the glory of God is quickly seen by even a cursory study of the gospel of John (see John 13:32; 17:1 & 5; 21:19). Is your devotion to God's glory as easily seen in your life by those on the outside looking in? Most believers pray something like: *"Lord, take all I am doing and bless it to your glory"*. This is little more than devotion to our own agenda in the hope that God will somehow bless it. In reality, what we should be praying is something like: *"Lord, take all that I am doing and eliminate everything that doesn't glorify you on your terms; and show me what You are doing so that I may do only what I see You doing."*

Holiness: Calling And Character

These, then, are the two sides of that personal holiness which God desires and intends in this season of spiritual awakening. It is the spiritual DNA He wants to impart into the House Church movement in this season. Separation and devotion. Character and calling. In this season of spiritual awakening God desires and intends to match our character with our calling. This is why many of you have been walking in a prolonged season of spiritual wilderness. Let me explain.

God often gives us our calling during some "mountain top" experience characterized by a deep sense of His Presence. But our character is nearly always the product of a wilderness experience where He causes us to walk through the valley of the shadow of death. Death to our dreams, our ministries, our comfort zones, our old selves. You never develop character (holiness) on mountain tops. God always builds character and holiness in valleys, in darkness, in trials, in loneliness and isolation. In other words, in the Wilderness. In God's economy of spiritual growth, the height of the tree must be matched by the depth of it's roots; and the height of one's calling must be matched by the depth of one's character. Tall trees with shallow roots will not survive the spiritual winds which are about to blow.

It was January of 1997. My wife and I were in Anaheim, California with friends from our church, attending a national conference at the Anaheim Vineyard (the last national conference John Wimber led before his home-going). On the last night of the Conference as we were leaving the auditorium our group paused to have our picture taken in front of the bronze statue of Jesus washing Peter's feet (which stood in the lobby of the building). One of our group asked a passer-by if she would take our picture. She agreed, and then added, *"I think the Lord has a word for those two"*, pointing to me and my wife. After taking our picture she came up to us and delivered a prophetic word about our future. It was our first real experience of prophetic ministry (and our first "drive-by prophecy"!).

As we left the building, openly wondering what had just happened, I turned to Gale and said, *"I think the Lord may be calling us back into full time ministry, but I just don't see how it will happen"*. Little did I know what God was unleashing that

Chapter 21 - A Bride, Holy & Blameless

night through that word, and what was about to transpire. I was in the international finance and investment business. Over the next three years it all collapsed. God took it all away and we entered into a wilderness of His design. By January of 2000 we were in bankruptcy and by March our 3,000+ square foot "dream house" on the Spokane River (it literally ran through my back yard) was in foreclosure. God had decided to teach me the lessons of humility and personal "death" the ol' fashioned way; by killing everything I had hoped to build.

We had left full time ministry after Seminary because we didn't want to "live by faith" any longer. Then, after bankruptcy and a total loss (our daughter had to finish her last year of high school by living with her grand-parents, while our son had to drop out of college and go to work - everyone having to grow up way too soon) the Lord asked us point-blank if we were willing to trust Him. Since the bankruptcy I had worked sweeping storage units to pay our storage bill, worked security for a local security firm (including three days of crowd security at a *"Three Days of Dave Matthews"* concert at "The Gorge" in George, Washington. Wahoo! That was fun!), and had served as interim pastor of a small Assemblies of God Church (that was more fun than a barrel of monkeys on caffeine!). But now God was calling us to once again "live by faith".

Gale & I agreed. Next, He sent us into the most drug infested neighborhood of our city to work with the most broken people we had ever met (In the immortal words of Mark Twain, *"It was no place for a Presbyterian . . . and I did not remain one for very long"*). He led me into a food ministry to provide a source of food to "the least of these" in obedience to Matthew 25:33ff. I used to have lunch with international bankers and financiers. Now God had me feeding the homeless in shelters (while fasting and praying for revival). We used to live in a dream house by the river. Now we were "technically" homeless (house sitting right now), living by faith as we wait to see what God will do next on this journey of faith He has us on. And, oh yes, He led us into the house church movement where I have become a perennial "thorn in the side" of anyone desiring to return to

Preparing For A Spiritual Outpouring

"the leeks, the garlic and the onions of Egypt". There is no going back. You will either perish in the wilderness, or you will allow the wilderness to do its work and prepare you for the next phase of your journey.

In short, God in His Providence has led us through *"the great and terrible wilderness"* where He has seen fit to confront and refine both our calling and our character. He has worked to remove us from all of our familiar comfort zones, to humble our pride, to confront our fears and to "kill" all those things we once held dear but which were unusable for His purposes. Why? In order to give us His vision for our journey, and to build His Calling and His Character in our lives. Separation from those things He cannot use and single-minded devotion to those things which matter to Him and Him alone. In other words, "practical holiness". Not a list of rules to be obeyed, but a passion for God that has become unquenchable.

If any of this sounds vaguely familiar in your own life, then the chances are good that you are in one of two places. Either you are presently in "the great and terrible wilderness" (see Deut. 1:19; 2:7; 8:15) where God is working out His "holiness" in your life, or you have emerged from the Wilderness and this letter is reminding you of what you have been through. If you are among the latter group, welcome to organic house church and to a place where God can use you in the coming move of His Spirit. If you are still among the former group who still find themselves in the Wilderness, here is my advice and encouragement: **Die Well**. Resist the sometimes overwhelming temptation to go back to the good 'ol days of Egypt: *". . . nor shall he cause the people to return to Egypt to multiply horses, since the LORD has said to you, 'You shall never again return that way.'"* (Deuteronomy 17:16). And don't try to get out of the Wilderness too soon. Give God the time and freedom necessary to complete the work He has begun in you. He wants to match your character and your calling, and that takes time. *"For they disciplined us for a short time as seemed best to them, but He disciplines us for our good, that we may share His holiness."* (Hebrews 12:10)

Chapter 21 - A Bride, Holy & Blameless

He is coming. Are we ready? Is your House Church a channel through which He can flow?

 Let the River flow!

Preparing For A Spiritual Outpouring

The Prophetic Time
In Which We Live

First Published December 7, 2009

22

"And of the sons of Issachar, men who understood the times, with knowledge of what Israel should do, their chiefs were two hundred; and all their kinsmen were at their command." (1 Chronicles 12:32)

According to the last enumeration of families found in Numbers 26:25 the tribe of Issachar consisted of 64,300 "families" (probably heads of households over age 21). It's easy to count heads. There are always plenty of them to count. But when it came to numbering those from among the heads who actually "understood the times" and knew "what Israel should do" the number quickly shrank, from 64,300 to 200. Followers are easy to find. But finding leaders who hear from God and who know what He is doing in their day and time is much more difficult. Just ask the famous sons of Issachar. The ratio there was 1 leader among every 321 followers. Finding genuine prophetic (or apostolic) leadership in our day seems even more challenging. And this leads us to the challenge of prophetic leadership in the Church today.

"The oracle concerning Edom. One keeps calling to me from Seir, 'Watchman, how far gone is the night? Watchman, how far gone is the night? The watchman says, 'Morning comes but also night. If you would inquire, inquire; Come back again.'" (Isaiah 21:11-12)

One of the great callings of genuine leadership in the Church is to speak prophetically both to the Church and to the surrounding culture. Isaiah, one of Israel's greatest prophets, spoke prophetically not only to the people of Judah, but also to Edom and the other people of the surrounding culture. When godly leadership speaks prophetically it continually finds itself struggling with two issues: the message on the one hand, and the timing on the other hand. To be meaningful, the delivered message must be spirit led, biblical and clear. In other words it must be focused and free of mixture (what I call being "spiritually clean"). Spiritually unclean words send confusing

Preparing For A Spiritual Outpouring

messages and spin people off into unintended directions. The Apostle Paul might put it this way: *"For if the bugle produces an indistinct sound, who will prepare himself for battle?"* (1Corinthians 14:8)

In addition to being clear, clean and specific, prophetic ministry delivered by leadership to the Church must also be timely. We need to know not only what God is about to do, but when He plans to do it. Prophetic ministry frequently views events through a telescope, causing the distant to appear close and immediate. In other words, prophetic ministry tends to confuse a telescope with an hour glass.

It is one of the great failings of the Church in our day that it has abandoned it's prophetic calling for a mess of therapeutic pottage. The Church has traded prophets for therapists with disastrous results. On the one hand, the therapists among us have replaced repentance with counseling. On the other hand, therapists bill by the hour which means there is no issue which can't be drawn out indefinitely. As a result, the Church has lost both the power of repentance and the urgency of the hour. The only thing we could possibly do to make the situation any worse would be to cover the whole mess with a superficial veneer of a "word of faith prosperity and healing message". But who in his right mind would be foolish enough to do that?!

Holiness, Judgment And "The Time Has Arrived"

For the past two (plus) years I have shared as often as possible regarding the clear prophetic words we received regarding God's desire and plan for holiness and fear, personal repentance and intimacy in the upcoming move of His Spirit. Let me be clear on this point. Any supposed manifestation of a move of God's Spirit devoid of these three characteristics isn't simply suspect. It is false. This week the "other shoe" fell. At a prayer gathering this week the Holy Spirit emphasized an additional aspect of the coming move: judgment. The theme of God's judgment is not new. I wrote about it in my house church equipping workbook *"A Kingdom, A People And A River"*:

Chapter 22 - The Prophetic Time In Which We Live

"I believe the Church in North America stands today between the book of Jeremiah on the one hand, and the book of Acts on the other hand. The great theme of Jeremiah is God's pending judgment upon Israel's unrepentant "spiritual adultery," whereas the great theme of the Book of Acts is the Pentecostal outpouring of the River of God's Spirit to empower the Church. Judgment versus spiritual outpouring; the two opposing yet complimentary sides of God's coming visitation. The tension between these two unfolding trends of God's activity will, in the years ahead, undoubtedly find expression in spiritual and cultural upheaval of monumental (even Biblical) proportions (consider for just a moment the changes which have taken place just since the events of September 11, 2001). Times of great revival often presage or coincide with times of great cultural upheaval and even judgment. It is like standing at the turbulent confluence of two great rivers. On the one hand, the River of God's Spirit, the River of Ezekiel 47, will flow in great power and blessing for spiritual renewal and revival the likes of which have not been seen or experienced in the West in well over 100 years. On the other hand, the River of God's judgment upon our increasingly "spiritually adulterous" culture is also preparing to flow in great power. One divine visitation with two powerful and different results. That is the challenge now facing the Church."

So, the word we received this week was not new. Rather, it was a strong and pointed reminder of what God had already told us. The power of these words and the seriousness of the choice which now lies before the Church quickly became very clear to all of us at the gathering. God is warning His Church (and all who will listen) that we now face a clear choice between pursuing His holiness (along with fear, repentance and intimacy) or experiencing His judgment. That's the message, like a spiritual bugle sounding clear and crisp, calling out to all who will listen and respond.

So, the remaining question has to do with God's timing in all of this. Earlier this week (yep, it's been a busy week) my wife (Gale) had a vivid dream that seemed to tie it all together. I asked her to write it up so I could share it here:

Preparing For A Spiritual Outpouring

*"In the dream, Maurice and I were on an island (I assumed it was Maui or like it) and we were receiving information that there was something coming - a huge wave was heading for the island and we were all preparing to leave the island. Maurice and I were in a car with other people heading up a road going up to higher ground. I looked out the window of the car and could see in the distance this huge wave with a big curl and white foam coming our way. It was still out quite a distance. When we got to the top, the others were getting out preparing to take a plane off the island. Maurice and I then went down the hill to where our house was and I proceeded to think through what we needed to take with us. I suddenly realized in the dream that I had bought 2 backpacks with wheels (which I actually did a couple of months ago) and thought that these would be just right to use to pack the essentials. I then went into the bathroom and started picking out a few things. I was methodically going through my makeup - picking & choosing items. Maurice was standing in the middle of the living room, waiting. I then asked him if he was taking anything. He said no, he didn't need anything. I said, "Aren't you even taking your tooth brush?!!" He said "no". So, I continued to pack just a few things. When I was almost finished, a small man dressed in a suit (he looked maybe Hawaiian) was walking through the house, passed by Maurice and then by me and as he approached the back door, he turned and said, **"The time is at hand"**, and he left. The dream was over."*

Please note the last statement (which I marked in bold): "The time is at hand". I'm willing to go out on a limb here and say, I believe we now stand on the eve of both spiritual awakening and judgment: ***"The time is at hand"***. The time for preparing is ending. The door is closing. The time of fulfillment is at hand. Are you and your house church ready?

He is coming. Are we ready? Is your House Church a channel through which He can flow?

 Let the River flow!

Signs, Wonders & House Church

First Published March 1, 2010

23

In my previous letter I came down pretty hard on what I regard as false "manifestations" or false signs and wonders. A reader responded as follows: *"Ok I get your point, this was a bogus instance of 'manna' etc. Are you saying that all reported manifestations of such things (gemstones, manna, gold dust) are also bogus?"* Good question, grasshopper. And when you can snatch the gemstone from my hand it will be time for you to go". Oops. Sorry. Old Kung Fu rerun just kicked in. It happens. Especially when I fast. I get delusional. Seriously, though, I have a couple of responses to this excellent question. But I am almost immediately skeptical of outlandish "manifestations" (I even left out the "angel feathers" incident). I am no expert (I only play one in newsletters) on supernatural manifestations, so I am in no position to say that all such manifestations are bogus. My friend, Jim Rutz, in his book "MegaShift" has documented numerous signs and wonders from around the world, including numerous resurrections from the dead. I have personally witnessed or experienced others: meetings where the overwhelming aroma of roses filled the room and made us all aware of Jesus' presence with us, angelic manifestations in gatherings. And, yes, we have seen healings, demonic deliverances . . and more. Been there. Done that. Profoundly touched by it. But experience can be an unreliable guide through the spiritual realm . Sooner or later (better sooner than later) we must all ask the question which leads to my next response, namely, *"What do the Scriptures teach us about the nature and purpose of miraculous signs and wonders?".* If Scripture and its clear teachings are not going to be your guide, then good luck in Wonderland, Alice.

Now, as we begin, allow me to interject a note of practical reality. It's impossible in one article of a few pages to exhaustively treat the biblical topic of signs and wonders. It is therefore the nature of the beast that I will pass over several smaller issues in favor of highlighting some broad principles.

Preparing For A Spiritual Outpouring

That doesn't mean that I am unaware of those details, but that I am choosing to focus on "the big picture" in this article. If I were to recommend a single book as a good overview of this issue, I would recommend Jack Deere's excellent book, *"Surprised By The Power Of The Spirit"*. While it is starting to show its age and while I don't agree with Deere on everything, it remains an excellent summary of the basic theological and experiential issues at the heart of this debate by a well trained theologian and practitioner.

Let's Start With Some Biblical Definitions

There are three specific terms used in the New Testament to describe miraculous signs and wonders, and a quick explanation of these words is a good starting point for our discussion. In the New Testament, a "miracle" (Greek: *dunamis*) refers to a work of God's power and emphasizes the supernatural nature of the event (e.g., the resurrection of Jesus is the pinnacle of all New Testament occurrences of dunamis). A "wonder" (Greek: *terata*) is that aspect of a miracle which emphasizes the awe-inspiring appearance of the event. This is best described as the "WOW!" factor. A "sign" (Greek: *semeion*) describes the fact that a miraculous event points to something greater than itself and emphasizes the purpose behind the event, namely, to communicate significant spiritual truth. Based upon these words (and verses which we will look at next) we could offer this summary statement regarding the nature and purpose of miraculous signs and wonders:

Miracles (*dunamis*) are signs (*semeion*) which cause men to wonder (*terata*), and which point to God at work, and are intended to result in repentance and faith.

Welcome to "Signs & Wonders 101". You now know more about the miraculous than most graduating seminary students do! And we're just getting started.

Chapter 23 - Signs, Wonders & House Church

Scriptural Guidelines Regarding Signs and Wonders

If the truth be told, I am what you might call a "biblicist". That should not be confused with a "bibliolotrist". A "biblicist" takes the Bible seriously. A "bibliolotrist" (yes, I just made that word up!) worships the Bible. I take the Bible seriously, but I don't worship it. I worship the God who inspired and wrote it. Being a biblicist means that when either my experience or my belief conflicts with Scripture, I assume that Scripture is right and that I am wrong until I can resolve the conflict. While I believe that my experience can sometimes "inform" my understanding of Scripture, it is ultimately Scripture which must set the boundaries of my experience and give it proper meaning. To misappropriate the words of Anselm of Canterbury (c. 1033-1109) in his famous maxim: Credo ut intelligam ("I believe so that I may understand"), I believe the Bible in order that I may understand my experience. To state this another way, the further away from Scripture my experience takes me, the more suspect my experience becomes. Like the Arctic explorer who drove a stake in the ground and attached a rope to the stake outside his tent so he could always find his way back in a blizzard, Scripture is our stake and rope amidst the blizzard of spiritual experiences afoot in the church today. Lose the stake or let go the rope, and the chance of finding your way home in the blizzard is doubtful at best.

I want to make it clear early on that I genuinely believe that the Church of God is, both in fact and in practice, a supernatural Church. The history or redemption is the record of God's supernatural acts to accomplish the redemption of His people. The Church is supernatural in the spiritual gifts which God continually and presently bestows upon believers, and the Church is a place where the "supernatural" occurs "naturally" as believers continue to touch and taste the powers of the Age to Come. So far as I am concerned, this is not a question of whether or not miraculous signs and wonders occur today. I am convinced by both Scripture and experience that they do. The questions which concern me have to do with God's purposes, man's "control" and our ability to exercise the spiritual

Preparing For A Spiritual Outpouring

discernment necessary to avoid getting deceived, disoriented and lost in today's "blizzard" of spiritual experiences.

The Purpose of Signs & Wonders #1: To Elicit Faith

John 20:30-31 - *"Many other signs therefore Jesus also performed in the presence of the disciples, which are not written in this book; but these have been written that you may believe that Jesus is the Christ, the Son of God; and that believing you may have life in His name."*

According to John, Jesus did "many other signs" which John chose not to record. But John chose to record seven specific miraculous signs in order to achieve a specific purpose, namely, to elicit and encourage faith in his readers: "that you may believe". The Gospel of John is built around seven "signs", beginning with the turning of water into wine at Cana in John 2 and climaxing with the resurrection of Lazarus in John 11. Each "sign" challenges those who experience or witness it to believe. Each sign is more complex than the one preceding it, and each sign is more polarizing than the one preceding it. And this is the two-edged sword of signs & wonders. They are complex and multi-faceted events through which God is at work doing many things at once. They are intended to elicit faith and repentance. But where faith and repentance are not forthcoming, they often result in hardness of heart and unbelief (more about that when we examine Hebrews 6:4-6).

The Purpose of Signs & Wonders #2: To Elicit Repentance

Matthew 11:21 -*"Woe to you, Chorazin! Woe to you, Bethsaida! For if the miracles had occurred in Tyre and Sidon which occurred in you, they would have repented long ago in sackcloth and ashes."*

This text in Matthew suggests that Jesus had performed "miracles" in both of these towns, but to no effect. The residents there did not respond with repentance, as they should have, or as Tyre and Sidon would have if they had experienced the same miracles in their midst. The strong implication of this verse is that miraculous signs and wonders have a purpose, namely, to bring about repentance in the hearts of those who witness or experience them. When the divinely intended response of repentance (and faith - see previous point) is not forthcoming, the result is hardness, unbelief and eventual condemnation rather than blessing.

The Sovereign Nature of Signs & Wonders

Matthew 12:38-41 - *"Then some of the scribes and Pharisees answered Him, saying, 'Teacher, we want to see a sign from You.' But He answered and said to them, 'An evil and adulterous generation craves for a sign; and yet no sign shall be given to it but the sign of Jonah the prophet; for just as Jonah was three days and three nights in the belly of the sea monster, so shall the Son of Man be three days and three nights in the heart of the earth.'"*

Religious leaders asked Jesus for a miraculous "sign" (semeion) in order to "test" Him. Jesus never gave into such demands or tests (although He performed many signs). Jesus is not a magician who performs on demand. He has no one whom He needs to impress. He is a sovereign God who always chooses the timing and circumstances of His signs. Please note: We don't choose, He chooses. You and I need to decide now who is sovereign - who is "in control" - when it comes to signs and wonders. If God is sovereign, then we will experience His miraculous signs and wonders in our ministries when He deems them appropriate and for purposes which please Him, not us. But if we are sovereign over signs and wonders then we are confronted with explaining why they don't occur whenever we demand or "proclaim" them (and they don't. Trust me.). If we are sovereign and in control of signs and wonders then it might indeed be possible to offer a "school of supernatural ministry" and teach people how to proclaim and perform. But if God is sovereign and in control then such behavior borders on "witchcraft" (see next section). Biblically speaking, signs and wonders are always a sovereign act of God. Sometimes He

Preparing For A Spiritual Outpouring

chooses to act in concert with our desires and prayers. Sometimes he chooses not to act, despite our pleas. The choice is His, not ours. Should we ask Him to act? Of course. Should we believe God for the miraculous? Yes! Should we expect God to act supernaturally? Yes! But neither our asking, nor our believing nor our expectations guarantee that God will move miraculously in any given situation. We must choose to obey; but ultimately He chooses whether or not to act. And that is a sovereign act on His part.

Power without Scripture = Witchcraft

Matthew 22:29 - "But Jesus answered and said to them, 'You are mistaken, not understanding the Scriptures, or the power (dunamis) of God.'"

Like the unbelieving Jews of Jesus' day who witnessed Jesus' signs and wonders, our failure to properly understand the Scriptures will result in our failure to properly understand the power (*dunamis*) of God, particularly as it relates to miraculous signs and wonders. Power is not its own explanation. Power requires Scriptural explanation. The fallen angels of the demonic realm wield supernatural power, but they do so apart from Scripture or any submission to God's authority. Simply put, spiritual power devoid of Scriptural obedience is magic and witchcraft. In his book *"When The Spirit Comes With Power,"* John White develops this idea further with the concept of "stolen power." White argues that all spiritual power derives from God. Here is what White says,

"There is one source of supernatural power, and one only. Satan's power is power once entrusted to him by God. God was the Creator of the power just as, being the Creator of all that is, he created Satan himself. The power was meant for use in God's service. It is what we might call embezzled power."

Lets be clear. All spiritual power originated in God. When Lucifer fell, along with a third of the angelic host, he and they retained the power that God had bestowed upon them in His service. Lucifer and his followers have now "embezzled" that power and use it to oppose God's purposes. God's power, embezzled and misused, now becomes "magical power." *"Whenever anyone, Christian or non-Christian, angel or demon, uses (God's) power for selfish ends . . . the power can be called magical power. It is the same power with the same characteristics put to a wrong use and subtly changed by that use. Christians who use God's power in this way have begun to act like sorcerers. Angels so using it fall."*

The Presence of Signs & Wonders Does NOT Equal Ministry Success

John 12:37-43 - "But though He had performed so many signs (semeion) before them, yet they were not believing in Him; that the word of Isaiah the prophet might be fulfilled, which he spoke, "Lord, who has believed our report? And to whom has the arm of the Lord been revealed? For this cause they could not believe, for Isaiah said again, He has blinded their eyes, and He hardened their heart; lest they see with their eyes, and perceive with their heart, and be converted, and I heal them. These things Isaiah said, because he saw His glory, and he spoke of Him. Nevertheless many even of the rulers believed in Him, but because of the Pharisees they were not confessing Him, lest they should be put out of the synagogue; for they loved the approval of men rather than the approval of God."

The presence of miraculous signs and wonders in our ministries does not guarantee that people will respond with repentance and faith (as God intended). In other words, the presence of the miraculous is NOT a "cure all" or "magic bullet" for all our ministry ills. In spite of the fact that Jesus performed "so many signs," many people still did not believe. Why? Because, according to Isaiah (and John) they were spiritually blind. And among the religious leaders who did believe on account of the signs, they still struggled in their walk of faith because "they loved the approval of men rather than the approval of God." My friend, Neil Gamble, rightly points out that *"The Israelites had everything that modern Christianity is*

Preparing For A Spiritual Outpouring

looking for while they wandered in the desert: the Glory, healing, all the gold of Egypt, clothes that never wore out, manna from heaven, fresh water with them all the time. (Yet) The bible says that they died in their sin". Neil believes their sin was their failure to achieve God's purpose in conquering the land. I believe it was deeper than that. Their sin was the sin of unbelief IN SPITE of being surrounded by God's miraculous signs and wonders! Don't expect signs and wonders to solve all your ministry problems. They won't. Some people will be touched and transformed by them (again, repentance and faith). But others will be hardened by them ("yet they were not believing in Him"). It was true in the life of ancient Israel, it was true in Jesus' ministry, and will be true in your ministry as well.

The Scariest Verse In The Bible

Matthew 7:20-23 - "So then, you will know them by their fruits. Not everyone who says to Me, 'Lord, Lord,' will enter the kingdom of heaven; but he who does the will of My Father who is in heaven. Many will say to Me on that day, 'Lord, Lord, did we not prophesy in Your name, and in Your name cast out demons, and in Your name perform many miracles?' And then I will declare to them, 'I never knew you; depart from me, you who practice lawlessness.'"

Personally, I regard this as perhaps THE scariest passages in the Bible. Here you have a group of professing believers (hey, they said "Lord, Lord") who have been prophesying, casting out demons and performing MANY miracles (*dunamis*). In other words, their ministries were characterized by signs and wonders. But on the day of judgment Jesus declares (the word is *homologeo* - "confess," which is found in Matthew 10:32. Ouch!) that He NEVER knew them and then commands them to depart. The usual approach is to interpret this passage to mean that these were believers who had never known Jesus "intimately" (the argument rests on the interpretation of the verb *ginosko* as meaning "intimate knowledge" which is a possible but not necessary interpretation). The problem is in Jesus response. His words, "Depart from me you who practice

Chapter 23 - Signs, Wonders & House Church

lawlessness," are a nearly exact quotation of Psalm 6:8 and Psalm 119:115 where the same words are spoken by God to wicked unbelievers! These false prophets were people who had become self-deceived regarding their true spiritual condition because they mistook the presence of supernatural signs and wonders as evidence of genuine spiritual fruit in their lives. This is why I included verse 20, *"So then, you will know them by their fruit"*. The context is how to know false prophets from true prophets. Jesus tells us that we will know them "by their fruit". Based upon the biblical context, I take this to mean that the presence of miraculous signs and wonders does NOT constitute genuine spiritual "fruit". Beware of judging the genuineness of your ministry by whether or not miraculous signs and wonders are present.

The 2nd Scariest Verse In The Bible (Hebrews 6:4-6)

Hebrews 6:4-6 - "For in the case of those who have once been enlightened and have tasted of the heavenly gift and have been made partakers of the Holy Spirit, and have tasted the good word of God and the powers of the age to come, and then have fallen away, it is impossible to renew them again to repentance, since they again crucify to themselves the Son of God, and put Him to open shame."

I believe this passage presents a "wake up call" to those who passionately advocate the pursuit of miraculous signs and wonders in their ministries (If the passage from Matthew 7 above hasn't already doused you with cold water). The occurrence of signs and wonders in the life of the Church represents those moments when people do in fact "partake" of the Holy Spirit and "taste" the powers of the Age to Come. The occurrence of signs and wonders represent a "kingdom break out moment" when the Age to Come manifests itself in power in the midst of "this present evil Age" and the Kingdom of God "breaks out" for all to see. At that moment the Kingdom of God becomes an experiential reality and people are called upon to choose faith and repentance over unbelief and rebellion. But this passage from Hebrews forces us to reflect upon a sobering reality, namely, there will be those who "partake" and "taste" but who walk away unchanged by the encounter. As I mentioned earlier, the Gospel of John demonstrates how miraculous signs have a two-edged effect. On the one hand they elicit faith and repentance in the heart of some; but on the other hand they result in unbelief and hardness of heart among others. These opposite responses to the same miraculous sign are best seen in the episode of the man born blind in John Chapter 9, and the raising of Lazarus in John Chapter 11 (signs 6 and 7, respectively). In a very real sense, the failure of signs and wonders to elicit faith and repentance can leave people in a worse spiritual condition than before.

All The Things I Haven't Dealt With

O.K., by now some of you are frantically trying to wrap your head with duct tape to keep it from exploding as you think about all the things I have "overlooked". Trust me, I haven't overlooked them. I've been ignoring them. So, consider this section the "lightning round" during which I will irritate you even further by quickly goring as many sacred cows as possible.

Issue: Didn't Jesus promise that signs and wonders would follow those who believe?

Answer: That depends. First, the passage from the Gospel of Mark (16:9-20) where this promise occurs (vs 17)is highly debated as to it's authenticity. It doesn't occur in the earliest manuscripts. Be careful about building a complete theology on a suspect passage. But, second, assuming it is genuine, what exactly does it mean? Does it mean that every time a Christian steps out in ministry the miraculous WILL or MUST occur? I don't think so, but you have to interpret this for yourself.

Issue: We just need more teaching on the miraculous. People just don't know.

Response: There is some truth here. Christians do need to know that signs and wonders are real, both in Scripture and in the on-going life of the Church. But you can't teach your way into the miraculous. I was once given "the tour" of a healing ministry by its founder and leader. He was quite proud of their training materials with their detailed explanations of the various Greek words for healing and disease, etc. Unfortunately as someone who majored in Greek in college and has taught it over the years, I can assure you that knowledge of the Greek does NOT lead to more healing, only to more misuse of the Greek. The Church in the West is led predominantly by teachers, and because of their gift, teachers never encounter a problem that they think can't be solved with more teaching (a similar observation can be made of all of the 5 fold gifts). But teaching tends toward "formulas" (obey these 10 principles and God will bless you in this area), and this includes healing formulas (which eventually lead to "schools" for the miraculous). The rude truth is that miraculous formulas don't work. Get over it or you will be either deluded or frustrated for the rest of your ministry.

Issue: *Didn't Jesus say we would do greater works?*

Response: Yes, He did: "Truly, truly, I say to you, he who believes in Me, the works that I do shall he do also; and greater works than these shall he do; because I go to the Father." (John 14:12) But here's the real question: "Greater than what?". For example, in Acts Chapter 3 Peter and John go to the temple and encounter the lame man at the Gate Beautiful. Now, have you ever asked yourself how many times Jesus had passed by that same man without healing him? But on this occasion Peter and John did something that Jesus did not do - they were used of God to heal this lame man. Was this a "greater work"? Or how about preaching a single sermon and seeing three thousand souls added to the Church on a single day? Jesus never did that. So, was that a "greater work"? And even the word "work" (Greek: ergon - literally "toil") isn't a normal description of something "miraculous,"although context can add that dimension. Be careful of reading more into a passage than is actually present.

Preparing For A Spiritual Outpouring

Issue: Didn't Jesus give his Church power over all the works of the enemy?

Response: Good question. Now we get down to the heart of the matter. Here is the passage most frequently cited for this: *"And the seventy returned with joy, saying, 'Lord, even the demons are subject to us in Your name.' And He said to them, 'I was watching Satan fall from heaven like lightning. 'Behold, I have given you authority to tread upon serpents and scorpions, and over all the power of the enemy, and nothing shall injure you. Nevertheless do not rejoice in this, that the spirits are subject to you, but rejoice that your names are recorded in heaven."* (Luke 10:17-20) The specific context here is the sending out of the 70. It is clear from the context that Jesus did indeed give those 70 disciples spiritual authority (*exousia*) over the power (*dunamis*) of the enemy. And this requires some explanation. First, note that it is authority in the name of Jesus. Simply put, it is about Him, not us. Unlike the seven sons of Sceva in Acts 19:14, we have been given the privilege of walking in the authority of the name of Jesus. Second, there is a difference between authority and power. Spiritual power (*dunamis*) and its exercise is something that God reserves for Himself. Sometimes He exercises that power directly, apart from any human instrumentation. Other times He exercises that power through human instruments of His choosing. But He always retains that power to Himself. The only Scriptural exceptions I know of are the angelic (and demonic) realm where God has imparted limited (but still profound) spiritual power to created beings which they can apparently wield. Even Satan and the demonic realm retain that *dunamis* which God entrusted to them when they were part of the angelic host. Unless you are an angel or a demon, you cannot claim the same power. Third, as believers, we walk in spiritual authority, but it is delegated authority. Jesus has been given "all authority . . . in heaven and on earth" (Matthew 28:18). When Jesus speaks, he speaks with the authority of the Triune God. When we speak, we speak with the authority of Jesus delegated to us as His sent-out Ambassadors. Our authority comes from a right relationship with the King. In and of ourselves, we have nothing. The spiritual realm understands and recognizes that authority, because they know Who He is and they know our relationship to Him (which explains why the sons of Sceva had no authority and paid the price for pretending - they had no relationship with Jesus). But power is not the same as authority. I know of no Scripture(s) which states that we have been delegated spiritual power (*dunamis*) or can exercise the miraculous power of God upon demand as we see fit. Even when Scriptures speak of miraculous signs and wonders being done by the hands of the Apostles, Scripture is equally clear that it is God Who is wielding His power, not men acting on their own. We see this clearly stated in Act 14:3: *"Therefore they (Paul and Barnabas) spent a long time there speaking boldly with reliance upon the Lord, who was bearing witness to the word of His grace, granting that signs and wonders be done by their hands."* Note that it was the Lord who was "bearing witness" and "granting that signs and wonder" should be done through the hands of the Apostles. Neither the Apostles nor their hands were anything. God was the one at work thru men.

Thoroughly confused? Good. Welcome to one of those "spiritual-truths-held-in-tension" which I spoke of last week in my "Apologia For Public Fasting". Attempt to resolve this tension in one direction or the other and the result will be either spiritual impotence and unbelief on the one hand (eg, "there's nothing we can do"), or spiritual witchcraft in the form of "proclamation" nonsense on the other hand. Accept this tension as a reality and you will discover the powers of the Age to Come being manifested in your midst as the Lord Himself "bears witness" to the reality of the Kingdom of God and grants that signs and wonders be done through you - as He chooses.

"Is That All You Want From God?"

In the year that D. L. Moody died (1899), at the end of a long and fruitful ministry of evangelism, he declared, *"Now the question is shall we have a great and mighty harvest or shall we go on discussing our differences? As far as I am concerned,*

Preparing For A Spiritual Outpouring

I am terribly tired of it, and I would like before I go hence to see the whole church of God quickened as it was in (18)57, and a wave going from Maine to California that shall sweep thousands into the kingdom of God. Why not?."

I began this discussion of manifestations and miraculous signs and wonders with an episode involving manna and gold dust. And I used that true episode as an exemplar of where the fascination with "signs and wonders" can lead the Church when discernment is absent. But I want to revisit that whole area for just a moment in order to offer some perspective and to ask a "bottom line" question. Let's pretend for just a moment that it is all true and that these are all authentic manifestations. My "bottom line" question is this: "Is that all you want from God?".

Let's reflect on that thought for just a moment. Is our hunger for God so shallow that it can be satisfied with trinkets and novelties. Are we "God chasers" or "trinket collectors"? And what if God in His infinite wisdom, love and power should choose NOT to heal those in your midst whom you and I believe need His healing touch? In our own fellowship I have witnessed perseverance and faith in physical suffering that requires a faith at least as great as any faith that heals. And yet God chooses not to heal (at least, not yet). And the impact of that faith on those who witness it is nothing less than profound. So which is greater, the faith to heal or the faith to persevere? And are you and I wise enough to make that choice in God's place? So whatever your desires and prayers regarding miraculous signs and wonders may be, I ask again, "Is that all you want from God?".

He is coming. Are we ready? Is your House Church a channel through which He can flow?

 Let the River flow!

Epilogue

"As spring-time precedes summer, and seed-time harvest, so every great onward step in the social and political progress of Great Britain has ever been preceded by a national Revival of Religion. The sequence is as unmistakable as it is inevitable . . . . Hence it is not necessary to be Evangelical, Christian, or even religious, to regard with keen interest every stirring of popular enthusiasm that takes the familiar form of a Revival. Men may despise it, hate it, or fear it, but there is no mistaking its significance. It is the precursor of progress, the herald of advance. It may be as evanescent as the blossom of the orchard, but without it there would be no fruit." (W.T. Stead, ***The Revival In The West***, page 33).

The Ordinary Versus The Extraordinary

Dr. J. Edwin Orr, the "dean" of revival students for over a generation, made a distinction between what he called "the ordinary work of the Church" in its daily ministry, and "the Extraordinary work of God" during seasons of revival. He compared the ordinary work of the Church with men drawing water from a deep well with a long rope and a lot of work. But the Extraordinary work of God in times of revival, he observed, was like a season of Monsoon rains when you're trying to figure out where you're going to put all of the water! This has been the historic experience of the Church during times of spiritual awakening for the past 500 years (since the Protestant Reformation). There is no reason to think that it will be different now!

As the quote from W.T. Stead during the Welsh Revival of 1904 indicates, some Christians are uncomfortable with the idea of "revival". When the spiritual outpouring of the Welsh Revival of 1904 reached America one Presbyterian publication noted, *"Theoretically, we are opposed to revivals and in favor of an even and uninterrupted growth of the Churches, but unfortunately, the facts are against us."* The facts were indeed against them and other opponents of revival. The reality was that roughly one-half of the membership of the Presbyterian Church in 1905, and an equal proportion of their ministers, had made decisions of faith during some prior revival (J. Edwin Orr, *The Flaming Tongue*, page 67).

What's The Purpose of "Revival"?

People opposed to the idea of "revival" (which I define as a season of divine visitation and spiritual outpouring) often ask, *"What's the purpose of a revival?"* This is a legitimate question which deserves a thoughtful answer. As we saw in Chapter 18 when we looked at Isaiah 63:15ff, there are times in the life of the people of God when the spiritual tide has gone out and no amount of human manipulation can disguise this reality or bring it back. It is in such times, when the people of God cry out in desperation, *"O that Thou wouldst rend the heavens and come down"* (see Chapter 19) that God chooses to act, both for our good and for His glory. Revival is what God does (in spite of our best efforts) to extend His Kingdom and to build His Church. And while He sometimes uses our "programs" for His purposes, more often than not He supercedes them . . . or ignores them altogether. I believe that God wants church growth and community transformation even more than we do. He just has a different plan for how to do it. God's plan is what I call "the desperation plan." God wants for His church to become so desperate that it is willing to acknowledge and own up to its own failure and spiritual bankruptcy so that when He moves to sweep people into His Kingdom and His Church the praise and the glory will belong to him alone. And that is the purpose of "revival"; to renew His Church and to extend His Kingdom in such a way that only He is glorified.

What Have We Learned?

Every person who reads this book with an open heart and mind will come to their own conclusions regarding what God is doing or is going to do in this coming season of spiritual outpouring. But to stimulate that thinking process it is only fair to ask ourselves this question at the end of this book: *"What have we learned about revival, and about God's plans for spiritual awakening in His Church?"* At the risk of being presumptuous

Epilogue

I would like to offer some thoughts by way of summarizing what I have learned over the course of several years.

Every Season of Revival Has A "Theme" Which Reflects The Heart of God For That Season. As an amateur student of the history of revivals since the Reformation, I have come to the conclusion that every revival of the past 250 years has possessed its own unique set of characteristics. Allow me to offer several examples:

The Great Awakening under Wesley and Whitefield (circa 1730 in America) was characterized by the return to an evangelical gospel, a call to personal holiness and intense ministry to the poor and destitute.

The Second Great Awakening in America (1795-1811) was characterized by large open air gatherings, quarterly communion meetings and powerful physical manifestations accompanying God's work among people.

The Manhattan Prayer Revival of 1857 was characterized by larger meetings devoted to prayer (which is why it was often referred to at "The Layman's Prayer Revival").

The Great Welsh Revival of 1904 was characterized in its early months by Evan Roberts and his "Four Points". Early in the revival, whenever Evan Roberts spoke he would emphasize four basic points. For example, during the first week of the revival, on Wednesday evening, November 2, he spoke at the Libanus Church in Gorseinon (Pastored by Thomas Francis). After the meeting closed, Roberts led a group back to the Moriah church for an "after meeting." There Evan Roberts declared, *"I have a word for you from God."* He proceeded to give them four points, which became the basis of all his revival work:

✎   1. You must confess all known sin to God, and put any wrong done to man right;

✎   2. You must put away any doubtful habit;

Preparing For A Spiritual Outpouring

✎   3. You must obey the Spirit promptly;

✎   4. You must confess your faith in Christ publicly.

These "Four Points" became the unofficial "spiritual theme" of the revival.

God's Unique Theme For This Coming Season. Now, I make this point for a specific reason. As you have read this book I hope you have noticed some emerging themes. I have noticed them over the years. Indeed, they have become more pronounced as time has allowed for prayer and reflection. I have come to the conclusion that God wants to place His unique "stamp" on this coming move by emphasizing these themes. I would encourage you to reflect on these themes as you read this booklet and ask the Holy Spirit to burn them into your own spiritual life:

1. Holiness & the Fear of God. I have come to the conclusion that God intends to bring His Church back to a place of walking in genuine personal holiness, the by-product of a renewed sense of the "fear of God". This is what I have come to refer to as an "Isaiah 6 experience" (See Chapter 14).

Holiness is that attribute of God's nature whereby He is totally and completely separated from sin and is singularly devoted to His own glory. Because we do not appreciate the holiness of God, we do not fear Him in a genuine biblical sense. The people of Israel discovered the fear of God when they stood before God at the foot of Mount Horeb in Exodus 19. Isaiah rudely discovered this fear when he was confronted in the Temple by a vision of God in all His terrible holiness (Isaiah 6:ff). That encounter with God's holiness transformed Isaiah. And Isaiah discovered what David meant when he wrote under the inspiration of the Holy Spirit, *"The fear of the Lord is clean . . "*. (Psalm 19:9).

The New Testament Church was rudely introduced to God's holiness when He struck Ananias and Sapphira dead where they stood for the sin of intentionally lying to the Holy Spirit (see

Epilogue

Acts Chapter 5) . The impact of that encounter with God's holiness upon the Church was profound: *"And great fear came upon the whole church, and upon all who heard of these things"* (Acts 5:11). God's holiness is not something to be trifled with.

2. Personal Repentance from Sin. A genuine encounter with God's holiness inevitably results in both "the fear of the Lord" and in genuine personal repentance from sin. I have come to refer to personal repentance from sin as *"the lost heart of the Church"* in our day. Generally speaking, personal repentance from sin is most lacking where believers have lost their sense of the holiness and fear of God. As Isaiah discovered in his temple vision (Isaiah 6), a genuine encounter with God in all of His "awful holiness" inevitably results in both fear and repentance on our part. Where repentance is absent among God's people, it is most often traceable directly to an absence of any genuine sense of God's holiness and fear.

3. Greater Intimacy With God. Any pretended intimacy with God that is devoid of holiness, that is devoid of the fear of God and that is devoid of genuine personal repentance is a farce and a sham, regardless of who is promoting it or claiming to experience it. The road to greater intimacy with God always leads through holiness, fear and repentance.

4. Service to "The Least of These". Genuine Biblical faith always expresses itself in Christ-like service to others, but particularly to "the least of these" (See Matthew 25:31ff). It is one of the outward manifestations of inward faith which Jesus specifically says will distinguish the believer from the unbeliever, the sheep from the goats, both now and on the Day of Judgment. In the coming season of Spiritual Outpouring, God wants His Church to return to it's roots of "faith expressed through service".

5. House Churches. It is not my goal to dismiss or irritate those believers who are committed to the organized institutional church. I was raised in it, came to faith in it, attended a denominational seminary, and served many years in many

Preparing For A Spiritual Outpouring

different capacities in institutional churches. So, I pray God's blessing on all that you do for the Kingdom. But in this new season God is looking for new organic channels through which the River of His Spirit can flow unimpeded by programs, politics or people who "don't get it". You cannot disciple the fruit of the coming revival by throwing them into a big box and plugging them into a program. For this reason (among many others) God is raising up the organic house church movement to be the new channel for the River of His Spirit.

Conclusion & Summary

A season of divine visitation is unfolding, a season built upon repentance, intimacy and holiness. Where it goes from here only He and He alone knows. He's God. We're not. Get over it! The River of God's Spirit, the River of Ezekiel 47, is preparing to flow in power . . . and holiness, the likes of which we have never seen before, at least not in the living memory of the Church. Are you and your house church a vessel through which He can flow? Are you pursuing repentance, intimacy and holiness? If not, now would be a good time to start.

He is coming. Are we ready? Is your House Church a channel through which He can flow?

 Let the River flow!

15354662R00103

Made in the USA
Middletown, DE
01 November 2014